Seven the *Times* SUN

GUIDING YOUR CHILD
THROUGH THE RHYTHMS OF THE DAY

BY SHEA DARIAN

San Diego

LURAMEDIA™

Cover illustrations by Mindy Dwyer
Cover design by Tom Jackson (Philadelphia)
Book illustrations by Cynthia Lair

Library of Congress Cataloging-in-Publication Data
Darian, Shea, date.
    Seven times the sun : guiding your child through the rhythms of the day / by Shea Darian.
        p.   cm.
    Includes bibliographical references and indexes.
    ISBN 0-931055-96-2
    1. Parent and child—Miscellanea. 2. Family—Religious life—Miscellanea. I. Title.
II. Title: 7 times the sun.
HQ755.85.D374   1994   93-46003
649'.1—dc20   CIP

Grateful acknowledgment is made for permission to reprint the following copyrighted material. Every effort has been made to trace the ownership of all copyrighted material. If any omission has been made, please bring this to the publisher's attention so that proper acknowledgment may be given in future editions.

Quotation from *Guerrillas of Grace* by Ted Loder. Copyright © 1984 by LuraMedia, Inc. Reprinted by permission of LuraMedia, Inc.
"Hanging Out the Linen Clothes" from *The American Songbag* by Carl Sandburg. Copyright © 1927 by Harcourt Brace & Company. © Renewed 1955 by Carl Sandburg. Adapted and reprinted by permission of the publisher.
"The Lantern Song." Copyright © 1987 by Leslie Poindexter. Words translated from German by Margaret Meyerkort. Reprinted by permission.
Quotation from *Our Inner Conflicts: A Constructive Theory of Neurosis* by Karen Horney. M.D. Copyright © 1945 by W.W. Norton & Company, Inc. © Renewed 1972 by Renate Mintz, Marianne von Eckardt, and Brigitte Horney Swarzenski. Reprinted by permission of W.W. Norton & Company, Inc.
Quotation from the movie *Parenthood.* Copyright © by Universal City Studios, Inc. Reprinted courtesy of MCA Publishing Rights, a Division of MCA Inc.
Quotation from *The Prophet* by Kahlil Gibran. Copyright © 1951 by Administrators C.T.A. of Kahlil Gibran and Mary C. Gibran. Reprinted by permission of Random House, Inc.
Quotation from *Stone Soup* by J.W. Stewig. Copyright © 1991 by J.W. Stewig. Reprinted by permission from Holiday House.

Portions of this book first appeared in *The Doula* and *Spiritual Mothering.*

For Morgan and Willa . . .
May you always walk through life
with celebration on the soles of your shoes.

The Sparrow, Sunday, with wings to fly,
One time the sun moves across the sky;
The Mockingbird, Monday, with wings to fly,
Two times the sun moves across the sky;
The Turtledove, Tuesday, with wings to fly,
Three times the sun moves across the sky;
The Whippoorwill, Wednesday, with wings to fly,
Four times the sun moves across the sky;
The Thrush, Thursday, with wings to fly,
Five times the sun moves across the sky;
The Falcon, Friday, with wings to fly,
Six times the sun moves across the sky;
The Sandpiper, Saturday, with wings to fly,
Seven times the sun moves across the sky.

Seven times the sun, Seven times the day,
Now the week is done, and the days fly away!
Fly away! Fly away! The days fly away!

Acknowledgments

I wish to thank . . .

*Those who were willing to read and comment on
the manuscript as it took form:
Tammy Corwin-Renner, Dan Corwin-Renner,
Rebecca Danica, Maggie Jezreel, Cynthia Lair,
Patti Smith, Mary Thienes, and
Debbie Westheimer.*

*My editors, Lura Geiger and Marcia Broucek,
who have been like faithful midwives
attending to the birthing of this book.*

*My partner in life, Andrew Darian,
for his assistance in research,
his encouragement, and
his willingness to carry out our family rhythms
through manuscript deadlines and re-writes.*

*And my daughters, Morgan and Willa,
for their patience in seeing this project completed.*

Contents

Preface

The Heartbeat of the Day

'As I watched the seagulls, I thought: 'That's the road to take;
find the absolute rhythm and follow it with absolute trust.''

— Nikos Kazantzakis

The Heartbeat of the Day

There is a rhythm pumping through every vein of the universe. Call it Divine Spirit, call it God, call it the creative power of nature. The rhythm is taken up by the sun, the grass, the children at play. Eternal heartbeat.

This rhythm is almost inaudible in the clutter and chaos of today. We experience a multitude of crises: the AIDS epidemic, drug addiction, the threat of nuclear war, environmental pollution, racism . . . the list goes on. No doubt our children live in a world of constant change and inconsistency. There is a call in the midst of the chaos to wake up to the beating of the universal heart. Uncover it and let it sound over the earth and through the cosmos! Let it restore to harmony all that has been disrupted: the rhythm of nature, the rhythm of peace among nations, the rhythm of human dignity and equality.

As a parent, there is much I wish to transform in the world. Yet I hear a nagging question as I scheme for a better tomorrow: How do I provide healing and protection for my children as they experience the uncertainty of today? Once again, rhythm resounds. The rhythm of family. Until we transform the chaos of family life, we can never hope to transform society. I envision a circle of caring intimacy. I envision a place where we celebrate waking, eating, noisy laughter, quiet moments of communion. I envision a sanctuary, however unorthodox, where each of us can develop inner harmony and strength of character. Perhaps from such a place we can more fully meet the world, sowing seeds of peace and understanding. The rhythm of family is a crucial catalyst in restoring the rhythm of the world.

What would it mean for a family to find "the absolute rhythm and follow it with absolute trust?" Years ago, if I had answered that question, my response would have produced images of boredom and limitation. Today, I delight in the knowledge that rhythm is a tool to discover freedom and celebration. Rhythm is not mindless routine. Rhythm is mindful awakening to the blessings we may find in our daily acts.

Most of us are familiar with the hurried and harried scenario of the morning race to beat the clock. Family members flying off in various directions, grabbing a "quick bite" on our way out the door to school or work. Try to imagine a scenario, perhaps less familiar, in which a family creates time to gather around the breakfast table. No one is reading the morning paper. They are reading the morning faces. Re-uniting after a night of rest. Making a place for themselves to witness one another's presence.

Within the flow of rhythm, there is time and space to know and see. Could this be why the thought of developing rhythm is uncomfortable for many of us? For if we say "yes" to rhythm, not only are we called to make a shift in priorities, we are also called to make choices and commit ourselves to carrying them out.

Recently, we have become painfully aware of the numbers of children who are raised in dysfunctional homes. For these children, inconsistency and disappointment are normal. How different our world would be if children were provided with an environment of stability and health from which they could learn to trust the world and their personal perceptions of it. I envision children growing compassionate and strong, able to meet the inconsistencies and conflicts that are an inevitable part of living.

When we guide our children through the circle of the day, we help them know they are supported on this earth by a Divine Spirit who is loving and dependable. The sun rising each morning, the stars coming out at night, the circle of a family gathered around a meal, the circle of childhood games . . . all of these allow a child to experience a sense of belonging. If we can learn to move with the rhythms of the day, we can help to hallow out a place for our children to find acceptance and joy. We can provide the gift of LOVING CONSISTENCY as a child's life unfolds. When we are able to give children the message that we celebrate their lives, it will be natural for them to do so.

When my life partner, Andrew, and I decided to conceive a child, I was working as a Protestant minister. Sadly, in my years of seminary training and church work, I had witnessed few families functioning in healthy, life-giving ways. Most of the clergy and lay people with whom I worked were experiencing deep confusion and brokenness in their family relationships. With trepidation, I decided to quit my job and prepare for the greatest challenge of my life: becoming a minister to my children. Fortunately, Andrew was able and willing to support us financially. He encouraged me to do the spiritual and emotional work necessary to become the kind of mother I desired to be for our children. Andrew dedicated himself to discovering the meaning of committed, nurturing fathering. We wished to enter parenting with our eyes wide open.

Our first daughter, Morgan, entered our lives screaming. She screamed for two months. She wouldn't breast-feed for weeks. Despite our plans and ideals, we suddenly realized how little in life we control. We became immediately familiar with the chaos of having a child in our family. Since then, I have often joked: "I used to be a perfectionist. Then I became a parent." Ah, how it stretches us. Parenting calls us to the center of the unknown. In the movie "Parenthood," directed by Ron Howard, "Grandma" offers an insightful analogy to a couple struggling with the dramas of family life:

"When I was nineteen, Grandpa took me on a roller coaster. Up, down, up, down. Oh, what a ride . . . I always wanted to go again. Ya know, it was just interesting to me that a ride could make me so . . . so frightened, so scared, so sick, so . . . so excited and so thrilled all together. Some didn't like it. They went on the merry-go-round. That just goes around. Nothing. I like the roller coaster. You get more out of it."

Perhaps there is a life we can discover with our children that has qualities of both the roller coaster and the merry-go-round. Andrew and I are striving to create a home in which we are comfortable meeting the unexpected joys, fears, traumas, and thrills of parenthood, AND we are able to establish a healthy family rhythm that offers groundedness and comfort. In this environment our family becomes a familiar circle where we can breathe and grow.

It is my hope that the resources offered in this book can be a tool to assist you in a similar journey. These materials reflect my bias for practical, accessible material to aid the complex task of parenting. I bring it to you in the attitude that the ideal picture and the reality of life can often feel as if they are on opposite sides of a wide ravine. I hope that these resources can help you to fill in that gap and bring moments of harmony and joy to your home. In this day, the Spirit knows we can all use more of this kind of peace.

Introduction

'I'll tell you how the Sun rose —
A ribbon at a time.'

— Emily Dickinson

How This Book Is Organized

Seven Times the Sun is a resource book offering parents a fresh view of daily life in the home and family. In each chapter you will find the following:

Reflections: These are brief anecdotes on the particular rhythm considered in each chapter (morning, mealtime, play, etc.). The purpose of this section is to invite you into the world of each rhythm. After you read each reflection, consider your own childhood memories and the feelings and images this time of day evokes for you.

Simple Rituals: The rituals in each chapter are simple ideas to help you celebrate the rhythms of the day with your child. A ritual is any act we come to with love and reverence, an action that sheds light on the sacred qualities of our lives. A ritual cultivates an attitude of awareness for creation's gifts. Ritual becomes part of a rhythm when it is consistent enough upon which to depend. It is this rhythmic approach to ritual that can be especially valuable in guiding children to meet the natural rhythms of their daily experiences with assurance and joy.

Passageways for Parents: These sections include insights concerning specific parenting issues that may affect a particular rhythm of the day. Effective parenting is cultivated through an ability to see the "bigger picture" of childhood and family life. As parents, it is helpful to create reflection time in which we may gain awareness and develop fresh approaches. When we foster clarity within ourselves, we are able to communicate more clearly with our children.

A Collection of Verses: A timely verse can create a bit of magic between adult and child. Children are drawn to the rhythm and rhyming of poetry. Most of the verses included are verses I have written for my own children or students I have taught. Allow these verses to be a "springboard" for your own creations. Become a poet! The verses you create for and with your child can make invaluable family treasures.

A Collection of Songs: Music can be a source of inspiration in the life of a family. If you are not musically inclined, it is never too late. Ask a musical friend to give you a few informal lessons to teach you some of the melodies in this book or make you a cassette tape so you can practice them. However you feel about your singing abilities, have fun! Then, at least your child may learn of the joy of music. Your singing is a valuable gift to offer your child, for the rhythm and quality of the human voice touches the heart in a way recorded music cannot.

Because pentatonic melodies are especially appropriate for young children, some of the songs in this book utilize the pentatonic scale:

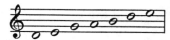

The pentatonic notes are indicated above the music for the convenience of those who play a pentatonic instrument. Since the voice is the first instrument a child develops, I prefer to sing a cappella with my children. This seems to allow for greater freedom and a more focused quality in our singing. However, chord symbols have been added on most of the songs (even if their pentatonic quality does not suggest our Western-style chords). In this way, these songs become approachable under a wider variety of circumstances. The chords might be especially useful for an older child learning to play the guitar or autoharp. For more information on the pentatonic scale, see "Songbooks" in the "Great Books for Parents" section of the Appendices (page 209).

A List of Children's Stories: The storybooks listed in each chapter illustrate rituals for celebrating the rhythms of the day and provide opportunities for enjoying the pleasure of the simple ritual of reading. Most of these books are what I believe to be some of the best of children's literature, reflecting — in text and artwork — a genuine reverence for life. I steer clear of the cartoonish drawings and superficial voice that are so prevalent in children's literature. Within the story lists, I offer an age-appropriate guide for ages 2 through 12. It is a broad guide that will be enhanced by your knowledge of your child's listening and reading skills and unique needs and interests.

A Tale to Spin: Storytelling feeds children's imaginations. The stories included in this book are folk tales from the Grimms' collection. I have retold these stories with an awareness for communicating a given "rhythm" reflected in each tale. It is best not to "moralize" about a tale or ask a child questions about a story you have told. Simply let the story speak to the child inwardly.

Storytelling allows us to experience the spoken word in a way reading from books cannot. When a story "lives inside" the teller, it has the potential to be communicated and heard at a deeper level. If you have never told your child a story "by heart," begin by telling a story from your own childhood. As you grow more comfortable, experiment with the stories in this book. Read a tale several times before you tell it in your own way. Don't worry about remembering the exact wording, but try to include all of the important elements when you retell the story to your child.

Appendices: At the end of the book, you will find an Appendices section that includes:

- Examples of Daily and Weekly Family Rhythms — for a more comprehensive, intentional approach.

- Great Books for Parents — on a variety of relevant topics.

- Resources for Parents — including parent groups, journals, and mail-order suppliers.

In raising my own children and collecting the material for this book, I have gained a great deal of insight from the approach of Waldorf education, based on the work of Rudolf Steiner, which recognizes and honors the importance of rhythm in the life of the child, in the classroom and the family. Although the material in this book is directed to parents, much of it can be used or adapted for the elementary, kindergarten, or preschool classroom.

If you are a teacher, my greatest consideration is to make available a practical, accessible, and creative resource that you can offer *to the parents* of your students. The holistic education of our children requires a collaboration between parent and teacher.

In guiding children, there are no easy answers, and we will be more effective teachers and parents if we can work together toward the beginnings of a common vision. It is my hope that in some small way, this book will be a catalyst for this work.

How You Can Use This Book

- **Take a look at your day.**

As you read each chapter, pause to consider how you now meet that particular rhythm of the day. Think about the daily acts that have become consistent. These could be as simple as brushing teeth before bedtime or eating lunch around noon. Are there favorite songs, circle games, or verses you and your child share? Are there any daily routines your child comes to with excitement or irritation? You may want to read only one chapter at a time and meditate upon that particular rhythm for several days.

- **Don't try to do too much too soon.**

Begin where you are, and when there are new rhythms and rituals you wish to bring to your child's day, choose one thing at a time. Too much ritual can become as chaotic as none at all. When you decide to foster a new ritual, choose something appropriate for your child's age and abilities and then allow the ritual time to become a rhythmic response. If you sing a new mealtime blessing, your child may not join in right away, but there is participation and learning in listening as well as doing. Since waking and bedtime are two of the most significant transitions for children, these are the rhythms you may wish to consider first. (For morning transitions, see chapter 1, page 25; for bedtime transitions, see chapter 7, page 133.)

- **Balance consistency with flexibility.**

You may want to decide on specific times for waking, mealtimes, bedtime, etc. If you plan a snack time mid-morning before your child's breakfast wears off, you could avoid an unnecessary cranky period. When you are consistent about a particular time for going to bed, your child will develop an inner rhythm that coincides. However, a schedule based solely on the clock can disrupt the kind of flowing rhythm that is most conducive to the growing child and healthy family life. There may be some rhythms (such as bedtime) that are scheduled by time; however, most rhythms can be associated with space and movement, rather than being dictated by the clock.

- **Allow for "breathing" room.**

Although intentional planning takes time and energy at first, after a few weeks you will find it makes your day simpler rather than more complex. Your creativity and energy will be fed by the rhythmic movements of the day. One helpful tool when creating daily rhythm for your family is to think of it as a "breathing" exercise. "Breathing in" is a time when one can focus inwardly and privately. This might include such activities as reading by oneself, stringing beads, resting, etc. "Breathing out" is a time of moving out to interact with the external environment. Such activities might include free-play with others, making a craft project together, visiting friends, etc. After an out-breath, an in-breath is natural and necessary. As in any relationship, a balance of intimacy and privacy, as well as activity and rest, is important. Remember to give both yourself and your child some "breathing room."

- **Even one consistent rhythm will help.**

In situations of divorce, in which your child goes back and forth between households, try to work together as parents to establish some rhythms that are the same in each household. Perhaps bedtime and the rituals around it could be the same in both settings. Even one consistent rhythm in a child's life will give the child a greater sense of continuity and security. In the same way, if your work schedule is sporadic and you are unable to establish rhythms at the same time each day, do the best you can. Perhaps you can create a ritual to honor being together after you return home. In your absence, timely rhythms might be carried out by a childcare provider.

- **Bring your individuality.**

Remember, this book is simply a guide for inspiration. It was written by a person who continues to learn daily about the complexity of parenting. Bring your knowledge, experience, and intuition to these pages. And, most importantly, bring your under-standing of your child so these rituals, stories, and songs may transform into a unique, creative dialogue between you and your child.

1 ▶ Greeting the Dawn
Celebrating Morning

'Full many a glorious morning have I seen.'

— Shakespeare

Celebrating Morning

I am not a morning person. Never have been. My daughters force me. Early, early wakers, ready to hug, eat, play, and argue hours before I would prefer to be called from my dreams. They are my morning mentors, teaching me to celebrate the new day. Darkness turns to light. Dreams turn to life. The glow of little morning faces (like the sunrise) can be missed if I tarry.

Dawn is an old, neglected friend. She arrives with full arms, bearing gifts without fail. There is a quality that fills our home in her first sheddings of light. A state of dreamy vulnerability as each of us finds our way into the world again. A tender time when our defenses have not yet reconstructed themselves. Our anger shows more easily, our delight, our affection. Sometimes we name the day in faith. Sometimes we doubt yesterday's brilliant plan. We may clear the way for the prospects of these moments. Creation is at hand.

When our second daughter was still nursing several times a night, for days I woke exhausted and irritated at the world. I decided for one week I would go to bed an hour earlier, wake before anyone stirred. Each day before sunrise, I would sit alone in the dark. I lit a candle, reciting a morning verse:

Walk softly toward the dawn,
Bow to the rising sun,
Breathe the morning,
Wake to the bright and early air.

In my meditation I called before me the images of each family member:

Andrew, my partner in life. Auburn hair. Dark, shining eyes. Gentle. Passionate. Dedicated father, lover, friend. Obsessive cleaner and launderer. Gifted teacher. Inspired handyman.

Morgan, our oldest. Brown bobbed hair. Grandma's greenish-brown eyes. Cherubic face. Strong. Deliberate. Intuitive. Compassionate. Dancer. Painter. Explorer of the world.

And Willa, our youngest. Ringlet curls. Dark, dancing eyes. Thin, strong body. Fiery will. Quick. Smart. Gentle singer. Wild pony. Catalyst of change.

In these pictures I saw clearly that my family deserves nothing less than to be greeted by me each morning with respect and gladness. I don't always live up to this knowledge, but at least I do more often now. That week, after my meditations, I crawled back into bed, waiting for the morning light to bring me close to those I love. And when it did, I opened my arms wide to receive my family . . . a new day . . . all kinds of possibilities.

Simple Rituals to Celebrate the Morning

From the World of Dreams To wake your child, think of alternatives to a noisy alarm clock or a loud voice: chimes, a bell, a flute . . . any gentle, celebrating sound to lull your child out of sleep. You may want to take a look at the "Resources for Parents" section in the Appendices (page 212) for distributors of instruments that the whole family can enjoy. As your child drifts from the world of dreams, avoid asking questions and keep conversation to a minimum for several minutes, so your child can get each foot planted firmly on the ground. Respect the time your child needs to make this transition.

Let the Sunshine In Choose a song or verse to enjoy as you and your child open the curtains or pull up the shades each morning. Gaze out the window or walk outside and observe the day's weather, the colors of the sky, the cloud formations, the way the grass and plants appear. Be investigators of nature together.

A Prayer Corner Arrange a room or corner of the house as a peaceful space for prayer. Each family member may want to sit in this prayer place for a few minutes each morning to meditate upon the day. Each of you can take turns decorating the prayer corner with such items as flowers, rocks, feathers, shells, artwork, or photographs.

A Box of Surprises On that weekend morning when you would like to sleep in, prepare a surprise box for your child. Set it beside their bed after they go to sleep. Fill it with healthy snacks, a library book, a simple craft project, love notes, etc. . . . If your child is old enough, agree on a "getting out of bed time" for this lazy mornin'. This could easily become a weekly ritual, hmm?

An Eye to the Sky

With an older child, plan an early morning outing to watch the sun come up. Find a place where the horizon is in clear view. Prepare food and clothing the night before. Think of songs and poems you can share to celebrate daybreak. Do a sun dance. Tell each other folk tales about the sun. Offer prayers in praise of this great light, and for the potential of the day.

Morning Bells

Acquire some finger cymbals or a percussion triangle for your child to ring to signal the new day, or look around your home for ordinary household items that make a pleasant sound. Experiment: tap the handle of a wooden spoon on the inner rim of a pot lid or the bottom of a stainless steel bowl . . . or perhaps you have a bell that is sitting idle that would make a friendly morning instrument. (You may want your child to be dressed and ready for breakfast beforehand.) This might be a fun way to signal your morning gathering as a family before everyone sets about the day's activities. As everyone gathers, perhaps each can name their hopes for the day, or you may simply want to gather in a circle and enjoy a few moments of silence.

A Parting Blessing

The way we depart from one another can affect our whole day. When family members leave for school or work, you can create a parting blessing to recite or sing together. You may want to use the "Parting Blessing" (page 32). A love-filled parting can go a long way over the course of a day.

Passageways for Parents: Morning

Children are sense organs, absorbing the sights, sounds, and textures of their environment. In the first seven years of life, it is especially important to protect children from the overload of stimuli so prevalent in our fast-paced society. Morning is a time to give this issue special consideration: What embraces my child in these waking moments? A blaring alarm clock, the morning news radiating from the radio or television, brash voices, people flitting this way and that? Or is my child embraced with gentle sounds, tender touches, a slow, rhythmic unfolding of the day that is predictable and familiar?

Think of yourself as a midwife, receiving your child from the womb-like existence of sleep. Children need to experience the tenderness of being welcomed into the world each day. Waking is one of the day's most significant transitions, as a child is lulled from the softness of sleep life into a world with sharp edges.

To facilitate a more peaceful beginning to your day, create a brief, personal meditation to do each morning before your child arises. Lie in bed and ease yourself into the world of the waking, or rise and sit in a special place where you have gathered some favorite photographs of your child or special gifts they have given you. Perhaps this could be a time to write brief notes in a journal to be given to your child at a future time. Envision you and your child moving through the day in healthy, vibrant, creative ways.

Create a pattern for meeting the world each morning. Your child will come to know the rhythm of the morning through your intentionality and guidance and will soon live out this rhythm with little assistance from you. Your family's morning may involve a special greeting or waking ritual, dressing, combing hair, eating breakfast together, and brushing teeth. If you find yourself rushed in the morning, find the will power to turn in earlier in the evening. I find that when I am rested, my parenting rhythms and intuition are indeed alive and well.

Verses for Morning

▶ *To Start*

The light opens up and I walk in,
The day invites me to begin.
I ask the day, "How shall I start?"
Says the day, "With a wish upon your heart."

▶ *Fading Dreams*

Fairies dancing on the lake,
In my dreams before I wake,
Fairies fade in sunlight rays,
Golden morning lights the day.

▶ *Morning Prayer*

I bathe in the dew at daybreak,
  sunlight crystals on my skin,
The humming prayers of creation
  can be heard in the morning wind.
I bathe in the dew at daybreak,
  as the wind combs through my hair,
and my voice rises up with the prelude
  of creation's morning prayer.

▶ *Walk Softly*

Walk softly toward the dawn,
Bow to the rising sun,
Breathe the morning,
Wake to the bright and early air.

▶ *Parting Blessing*

Open wide the door to morning,
Take love as you depart;
Walk gently on the earth,
With kindness in your heart.

Open wide the door to morning,
Take courage as you go;
Stand for the small and helpless,
Work for the good to grow.

Open wide the door to morning,
Take beauty as a clay
And mold an act of thankfulness
For the blessing of this day.

We Turn Again to the Sun

Brightly

Shea Darian

We turn a - gain to the sun. A - rise ev' - ry
one. We'll o - pen our eyes to greet the day,
O - pen our hearts to work and play, O - pen our lives and begin to sing of all this day will bring.

Good Morning to You

Joyfully

Shea Darian

Parent:
Good morn-ing, good morn-ing, good morn-ing to you.

Child:
Good morn-ing, good morn-ing, good morn-ing to you.

Unison:
Good morn-ing's what we say, good morn-ing's what we do. Good

morn-ing, good morn-ing, good morn-ing to you.

Morning Comes Early

2-part round

Slovakian Folksong

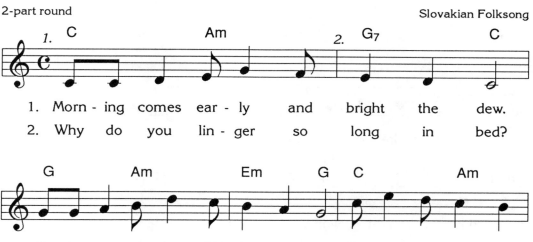

1. Morn - ing comes ear - ly and bright the dew.
2. Why do you lin - ger so long in bed?

Un- der your win- dow I'll sing to you. Up then, my com-rades,
Op- en your win- dow and show your head. Up then with sing - ing,

up then, my com-rades; Let us be greet-ing the morn so new.
up then with sing - ing; O- ver the mead-ow the sun shines red.

Sun, Wake Up

Brightly

Morgan* and Shea Darian

Sun, wake up, it's time to talk a - bout an - o - ther day. _____ I won - der what your light will bring, what gift your gold - en ray. _____ Shine up - on the sing - ing, shine up - on the dance, shine up - on my wind - ing way. Sun, wake up, it's time to talk a - bout an - oth - er day.

*This song came spilling out of my daughter Morgan as she played outside in the sun one morning.

Joy Comes in the Morning

3-part round

Shea Darian

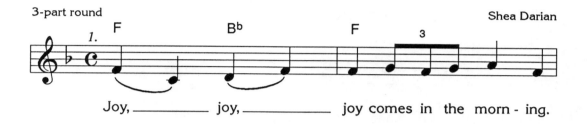

Joy, _____ joy, _____ joy comes in the morn - ing.

Joy, _____ joy, _____ joy _____ comes.

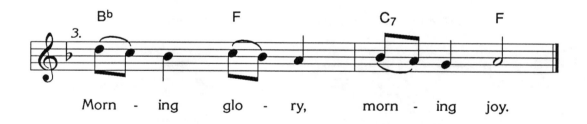

Morn - ing glo - ry, morn - ing joy.

Song to the Sun

Moderately

Zuni Song

Wake! A-wake! A-wake! Wake! A-wake! A-wake! The sun has come and the moon has gone, We greet the sun with our morn-ing song. We are thank-ful for an-oth-er day, We are thank-ful for an-oth-er day.

Wake! A-wake! A-wake!

Wake! A-wake! A-wake!

Stories for Morning

Busy Monday Morning by Janina Domanska .... (2 - 7)
> A translation of a Polish folk song from the author's childhood. Reveals parent and child working side-by-side in the fields each morning of the week. Complete with musical score. (New York: Greenwillow Books, 1985)

I Am Eyes, Ni Macho by Leila Ward .... (2 - 8)
> Simple text and soothing illustrations celebrate a child's morning greeting to the world. "Ni macho" is an expression in Swahili to announce waking up to the world. It means "I am eyes" and is a reminder to absorb the day's natural beauty. (New York: Scholastic, Inc., 1987)

When the Sun Rose by Barbara Helen Berger .... (2 - 8)
> With the rising of the sun, a little girl is visited by a special friend. Beautiful images of the sun's light and warmth. (New York: Putnam Publishing Group, 1986)

The Way to Start a Day by Byrd Baylor .... (4 - 12)
> A celebration of the sun that offers sun rituals from around the world. (New York: Macmillan Children's Book Group, 1978)

Morning Milking by Linda Lowe Morris .... (5 - 10)
> A child goes out to help her father milk the cows each morning on the family dairy farm. She soaks in the sights, sounds, and feelings of the morning and wishes she could make time stand still in the beauty of these early morning moments. (Saxonville, MA: Picture Book Studio, Ltd., 1991)

A Morning Tale to Spin

"A Riddling Tale"

Once there were three women who were turned into flowers. They grew side-by-side in a meadow. Each one looked exactly like the other two. But at night one of the flowers changed back into a woman, and she could go home to spend the nighttime hours with her family.

Before sunrise one morning, she turned to her husband and said: "Come and pick me after sunrise this morning. This will break the spell, and I will be set free."

And that is what the husband did. And the woman was indeed set free. So they lived happily by night and by day.

The riddle, if you care to try it, is this: Remembering that the three flowers looked exactly alike in every way, how did the husband know which flower to pick?

The answer, quite simply: Since the woman was at home and did not spend the night in the meadow with her friends, she was the only flower upon which the dew had not fallen. Her husband recognized her easily.

(A Grimms' tale, retold by Shea Darian)

2 ◗ 'Round the Table
Celebrating Mealtime

⁶Never had the villagers shared such a feast.
Never had they tasted such soup.
And imagine, made from a stone!
They ate and drank, and after that they sang and danced.⁹

— Stone Soup, as retold by J.W. Stewig

Celebrating Mealtime

I remember, at five years old, stretching to see the plate of my bedroom light switch. I knew the words by heart: "The family that prays together stays together." Beneath the message appeared a black-on-white silhouette of a family seated around a kitchen table graced by mounds of steaming food. Heads bowed and hands clasped in gestures of prayer.

This memory flooded over me as our family held hands around the dinner table and bellowed an energetic version of the folk tune "Johnny Appleseed":

> *"Oh, God is good to us*
> *And so we thank you, God*
> *For giving us the things we need*
> *The sun, the rain, and the appleseed*
> *Oh, God is good to us."*

Our daughter Morgan was hanging on every word, captivated by the irresistible mixture of worship and fun. Andrew glanced warmly at Willa, our youngest, who was swaying to the lilting melody. I was overcome with the power of the prayer, unorthodox as it may have been.

Suddenly I longed to transport myself back into my five-year-old body. I wanted to run into the kitchen and find my childhood family, ready to indulge in a pot of black-eyed peas and Mom's best corn bread. I wanted to take hands in a circle and bellow out a chorus of "Johnny Appleseed" with enough fervor to remind us that our gathering was a living sacrament. I wished for some magical way to reach out to my childhood family with healing to transform their struggles, with reason to uphold their joys.

To "stay together" as a family means more than being in the same place at the same time. Staying together means supporting and honoring one another. It is this kind of "staying power" that can be fostered by the tool of collective prayer. When we enter into prayer together and recognize the Divine Spirit among us, the effect is liberating. We can no longer ignore that our relationships have eternal consequences.

I have discovered the blessing of our meals to be as important as the feasting. Our familial affection is fertilized as we open ourselves to the gifts of food and companionship. "Saying grace" becomes an invitation for showing grace to all around the table.

And 'round this table we meet again and again, inviting others to join us. Sometimes in person. Sometimes in prayerful thought. I may not be able to transport myself into that five-year-old body, but I can welcome my first family to this present circle of love. In person. In Spirit. No matter. Mealtime sacrament is far-reaching and curative.

Simple Rituals to Celebrate Mealtime

Lift Every Voice

Mealtime is an opportunity to voice our prayers in one another's presence. You may wish to memorize short poems and verses to recite together. Children will learn these by hearing them from day to day. If you use a new blessing for several days, it will be more easily absorbed. Think of blessings and songs you learned as a child and consider passing them on. Many of the songs that follow me from childhood are old church hymns I learned from my mother and grandfather. One that I remember fondly has become a mealtime prayer for us: "For the Beauty of the Earth" (page 54). If you have a preference for spontaneous spoken prayers, be sure every family member who is able and willing has an opportunity to offer these. Offering prayers for one another in this way can inspire intimacy. Children will know their personal prayers are worthy of being spoken and heard, and you will be enlightened by their contributions.

Candlelight Dinner

A few moments of silence at mealtime can be worth a thousand words. Silence is especially effective in the throes of a hassled or busy day. Light a candle. Hold hands and observe silence. You might want to begin and conclude these moments of silence with one of the sentence prayers included in "Verses for Mealtime" (page 48).

The Gift of Prayer

Mealtime prayers can be an inspiration for creating unity and solidarity in your family circle. Writing original prayers as a family can be a fulfilling group endeavor, or you may want to offer original prayers as gifts for one another. If someone in your family does most of the cooking, it may be a habit to expect it. Write a blessing that offers thanks for the handiwork of the cook. If your child is old enough to participate, each week take turns bringing a short devotional passage on love, thankfulness, unity, etc., to read. For a younger child, bring a short mealtime story each week, perhaps for a special weekend meal. (Try "The Magic Porridge Pot," page 57.)

A Food Journey

With your child, trace the journey of a food on your table. Where and how did the food grow? Who grew it? How did it get to the store and to your kitchen? Was it grown in your own garden? Who prepared it for eating? Children develop a new appreciation for food if they can have a little garden patch during the growing season to grace your table with all kinds of vegetables and fruits. If you have never gardened before, you might want to find an experienced organic or bio-dynamic gardener nearby who can give you some tips. Also, check out books on gardening in the "Great Books for Parents" section of the Appendices (page 206).

Places, Please

For a special occasion cut out place mats from some heavy, light-colored paper. Have your child decorate them with crayons or colored pencils and place them around the table. Perhaps each person's name and a short verse could be written on them. This is a good way to create peace in the kitchen while finishing up preparations, and your child will enjoy bringing a special part to the festivities.

Circle Prayers

A simple participatory prayer is the circle prayer. At breakfast someone might begin: "Spirit of Life, bless the activities of our day." The prayer travels around the table as each person names a special event, work to be accomplished, time with a friend, etc. For a Thanks-giving meal, someone might begin: "Creator, we offer thanks for the blessings of our lives." The prayer comes full circle as each person names a blessing from the year past for which they wish to offer thanks.

Food for the Hungry

Create a hunger bank, perhaps by decorating a can with a resealable plastic lid. Set it on your table to collect money for an organization that feeds hungry people. Perhaps once a week, you will want to bring offerings for your hunger bank and share a special blessing for those who do not have enough food to eat.

Giving and Receiving

During prayer, hold hands with right palm downward in a gesture of giving, left palm upward in a gesture of receiving. Your child may be too young to consciously understand the symbolism, but the positive energy that is created by the gesture will be intuitively felt.

Out and About

When you are running errands or visiting someone, mealtime may creep up on you. Before you leave home, pack a basket with food that is easy to eat "on the go." Your child will enjoy preparing the basket with you, and this will save you from those intensely frustrating moments when you are stranded somewhere with a hungry, whining child and no food to offer. Bring a jar of water along and a blanket, if the weather will allow a picnic.

Shake the Pans

Family teamwork may be inspired by cooking and washing dishes with one another. Plan a family potluck for which each family member prepares one dish to enjoy. You may wish to decide who will prepare the main dish, a vegetable, a salad, a dessert, etc. Children's cookbooks are handy for gathering ideas for cooking with children. An older child may be given the task of cooking an entire meal for the family once or twice a week. When it is time to clean the kitchen, divvy up the tasks that need to be done. Perhaps one person washes dishes, one rinses (or stacks them in the dishwasher), one puts leftovers away, one sweeps or mops the kitchen floor, etc. Singing can turn your work into a playful frolic.

Passageways for Parents: Mealtime

Particular foods create particular rhythms in our bodies. Take responsibility to learn about healthy nutrition. Take note how particular foods affect your individual family members by keeping a journal over a period of several weeks. Older children may wish to keep their own journal, while you may do so for a younger child. Note what foods are consumed, and keep a running record of your child's physical, emotional, and mental state. Look for connections between what your child eats and how your child is feeling. Food allergies, additives, a deficiency of a vitamin or mineral, over-consumption of a particular food (such as red meat), processed sugars, and the like can play havoc with a child's growth and well-being.

As parents, we have a great deal of influence over our young children's eating habits — more than most of us like to admit, because it might mean transforming our own eating habits as well. Older children in particular can be influenced, not by nagging, but by uncovering information about the effects of particular foods on our bodies and on the world. As you take a closer look at the foods you eat, uncover the implications of your eating habits. Ask yourself: What makes up the bulk of our diet? Are the foods we eat highly processed? Are they grown with chemicals and pesticides? Or produced by companies that exploit their workers? How do the foods we eat and the packaging they come in affect the earth, animal life, our bodies? Is buying healthy foods, which may cost more, a worthy sacrifice in working toward healthy bodies and a healthy planet?

To enhance your family's diet, you may wish to grow your own fruits and vegetables, find an organic farmer nearby, join a natural food co-op, or find a buyer's club where you can buy healthy foods in bulk. Do not be deceived by the "healthy" label, however; you still have to read labels — even at the health food store.

One of the most comprehensive, accessible, family-centered approaches I've found to many of the above questions is Cynthia Lair's book, *Feeding the Whole Family*. For further resources on food and your family's well-being, consult the "Cooking & Nutrition" listings in the "Great Books for Parents" section of the Appendices (page 205).

Verses for Mealtime

▶ Love-feast

We gather 'round this table,
Where bodies are renewed,
Where hearts appease their hunger,
For we feast on more than food.

▶ From Little Bursting Seeds

The seed and root beneath the Earth,
the willful, growing shoot . . .
the hopeful bud, flow'ring blossom
turned to glowing fruit.

We thank the Earth who grew this food
from little bursting seeds,
and the Keeper of the Earth,
whose gifts fulfill our needs.

▶ Family Blessing

We are humbled in our questing,
as we open to receive,
We're a family changed and changing
by the tapestry we weave.

▶ Blessing for the Gardener

A garden's bounty before us . . .
We thank the gardener's hands,
that tilled the earth, that planted seed,
that nurtured the plentiful land.

❱ *Sentence Prayers*

Rest and be thankful.
> — *Inscribed on stone seat in the Scottish Highlands*

Now join your hands, and with your hands your hearts.
> — *Shakespeare*

Blessings on our meal and peace on the earth, the home for all.
> — *Adaptation of a common "Waldorf" blessing*

Songs for Mealtime

Peace Blessing

Prayerfully

Shea Darian

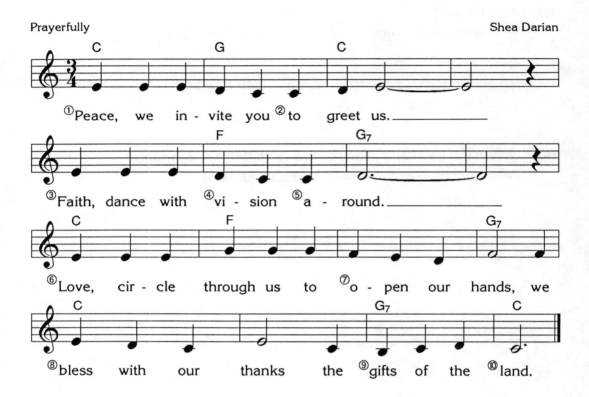

①Peace, we in - vite you ②to greet us.

③Faith, dance with ④vi - sion ⑤a - round.

⑥Love, cir - cle through us to ⑦o - pen our hands, we

⑧bless with our thanks the ⑨gifts of the ⑩land.

Hand Movements (flowing and worshipful):

Numbers correlate to the beginning of each gesture.

① Peace: begin with palms together in a gesture of prayer, chest height. Raise hands straight up in front of face to above head height, as you sing.
② To: separate hands, turning palms toward you. Bring down slowly to sides of face.
③ Faith: criss-cross hands in front of eyes and back to sides of face.
④ Vision: gradually lowering hands, criss-cross in front of chin and back out.
⑤ Around: criss-cross hands in front of chest then back out and around, creating a circle with your hands and arms in front of you.
⑥ Love: close hands in gentle fists, and circle each around the other as you bring hands toward your chest.
⑦ Open: opening hands with palms facing up, swing hands to elbow height and shoulder width.
⑧ Bless: bring open palms to lay criss-crossed on chest, right over left.
⑨ Gifts: right hand swings out in front, palm up. (Hold for #10.)
⑩ Land: left hand swings out in front, palm up.

Circle of Friends

4-part round

Adaptation of "Dear Friends"*

Cir - cle of friends I love, Let me tell you how I___ feel: You have gi - ven me such___ treas - ures, cir - cle 'round a - gain.

*The original version of "Dear Friends" and other rounds sung to this melody may be found in *Rise Up Singing*, listed in the "Great Books for Parents" section of the Appendices under "Songbooks" (page 209).

A Gnome in the Garden

Gently

Shea Darian

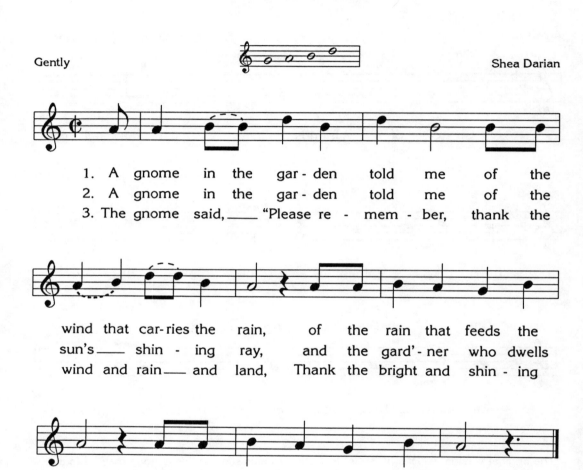

1. A gnome in the gar - den told me of the wind that car - ries the rain, of the rain that feeds the earth, of the earth that holds the grain.

2. A gnome in the gar - den told me of the sun's___ shin - ing ray, and the gard' - ner who dwells there work - ing pa - tient - ly to - day.

3. The gnome said,___ "Please re - mem - ber, thank the wind and rain___ and land, Thank the bright and shin - ing sun and the gard' - ner's tend - ing hand."

Prayer of Gratitude

Reverently

Shea Darian

We thank the Cre-a-tor for the har-vest of the earth, We

thank the ___ earth for its food, We

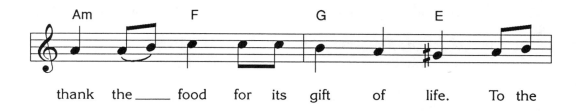

thank the ___ food for its gift of life. To the

one who pre-pared it, we give our gra-ti-tude.

For the Beauty of the Earth

Words by Folliot S. Pierpoint
(slightly revised)

Music by Conrad Kocher
Arranged by H. Monk

1. For the — joy of hu - man love, Bro - ther, sis - ter,
2. For the — beau - ty of the earth, For the glo - ry

par - ent, child, Friends on — earth and friends a - bove,
of the skies, For the — love which from our birth

For all gen - tle thoughts and mild; Love Di - vine, to
O - ver and a - round us lies; Love Di - vine, to

thee we raise This our hymn of grate - ful praise.
thee we raise This our hymn of grate - ful praise.

We Thank Thee

4-part round
Traditional Text

Shea Darian

Thou   art   great   and   thou   art   good,

And   we   thank   thee   for   this   food.

Stories for Mealtime

Pumpkin, Pumpkin by *Jeanne Titherington*   (2 - 7)

A simple story about a boy who grows a pumpkin. The beautiful illustrations follow a pumpkin's growth from seed to harvest, and back again. (New York: Greenwillow Books, 1986)

Stone Soup *retold by John Warren Stewig*   (3 - 10)

A recent version of a classic tale. Grethel and her mother make a poor living. Grethel leaves home one day to "discover a way to make life easier." She finally comes to a village, weary and hungry. The villagers will not share their food with her, so she devises a plan to persuade them. And imagine, all from a stone! (New York: Holiday House, Inc., 1991)

Half a World Away by *Arlette Lavie*   (4 - 10)

An allegory about a land suffering from the hunger and sickness created by a mysterious purple cloud. The children who live in another land where there is an overabundance of food and resources bravely persuade their parents to petition their government to act. (New York: Child's Play (International) Ltd., 1990)

White Wave, *a Chinese tale retold by Diane Wolkstein*   (4 - 12)

A gentle tale from the Taoist tradition. A hard-working farmer finds a white shell on his way home from the fields one day. After that, he mysteriously finds dinner cooked and ready for him on his table each night when he returns home. The secret of the white shell transforms his life. (New York: Harper Collins Children's Books, 1979)

"The Food," an excerpt from **The Indian Way** by *Gary McLain*   (8 - 12)

With each full moon, Grandpa Iron, a Northern Arapahoe medicine man, gathers his grandchildren and tells them a story about communing with Nature. This story focuses on having respect for living things, never taking more food than we need, and thanking the animals and plants who provide the food. (Santa Fe: John Muir Publications, 1990)

A Mealtime Tale to Spin

"The Magic Porridge Pot"

In a village near the edge of a forest, there lived a little girl and her mother. They were very poor and often ate only nuts and berries they found in the forest. One morning as the girl was picking wild blackberries, she turned to see an old woman coming toward her with a small iron cooking pot. The old woman smiled kindly and said: "Listen carefully, and do as I say. Take this pot home to your mother. Whenever you are hungry, say to the pot, 'Cook, little pot,' and it will bubble up with good, sweet millet porridge. Then, when you have had your fill, say to the pot, 'Cease, little pot,' and it will stop cooking."

The child thanked the old woman for such a fine gift and hurried home to show her mother. In the days to come, they grew healthier and happier, for they could eat sweet millet porridge whenever they wished. When they were hungry and they wanted the pot to cook, they said, "Cook, little pot," and when they had eaten their fill, and they wanted the pot to stop cooking, they said, "Cease, little pot."

Late one afternoon, the little girl was away with some friends, and the mother grew hungry. She peered into the little pot, thankful as always, and said, "Cook, little pot." Right away, the pot bubbled up with the sweet millet porridge, and she had a fine meal of it. But when she wanted to tell the pot to stop cooking, she couldn't remember the right words to make the pot stop. She said, "Stop, little pot!" and "That's enough, little pot!" and "Be done, little pot!" Well, of course, the pot went right on cooking. The porridge bubbled up over the sides of the little pot, but the pot didn't stop. It bubbled onto the floor, ran out the door and into the next house and the next. The pot cooked and cooked as if it wanted to feed everyone in the village.

Now, the poor people were happy to see such a great amount of food before them. They ate and ate the sweet porridge. But soon people became greatly worried, for the porridge was filling up their homes, their roads, and their entire world. They didn't know what to do. Then, finally, the little girl saw what was happening. She made her way home and said to the pot, "Cease, little pot!" The pot stopped cooking, but anyone traveling that evening had to eat their way through the porridge.

(A Grimms' tale, retold by Shea Darian)

3 ◗ Come, Play With Me!
Celebrating Play

'The little ones leaped, and shouted, and laughed
And all the hills echoed . . . '

— William Blake

Celebrating Play

The alley transforms into a soccer field. A half-dozen children indulge in a heated game. No rules. No score. They play until it isn't fun. The ball ricochets off a garage and bumps a child in the head. High drama: her eyes roll back, her legs stagger, her body collapses in a heap. Then she rises to peels of laughter. A dozen hands and feet scramble for the ball. A door slams! All eyes dash to the old man's back door. His deep voice digs into the abrupt silence: "Go play where you live," he yells, "Go play where you live!" Halfway to his back gate, arms flailing, he shoos away the breeze more than the children. A giggle sends arms and legs flying again toward the ball. The old man totters back into his house as quickly as he came. He leaves the children to their afternoon. Until the next time. The children will expect him.

Child-energy can be disturbing. It grabs at our middle, threatens to be infectious, tempts us to run and jump into it headlong. The old man heard the child-energy tapping at his window, blowing in under the door. Perhaps the old man's habit of interference was the only way he knew to become part of it. We are susceptible. We are the big, serious children. We cannot ignore that faint child-voice within us calling, "Come play with me!" We put it down fast. "Go play where you live!" we yell. We send the sulking child back to some distant place where there was time to spare. Was there ever time to spare?

I have known my friend Maggie since we were seven years old. I remember her then as a priestess of play. She always had the secret of some adventure in her eyes. The summer we were twelve, Maggie took me to "the trestle," a railroad bridge built over a moderate river stream that became the host of a chain of childhood memories. To us, it could have been the Mississippi. When we were twelve, we were so impressed by the possibilities that little river held, we did not see it in realistic proportion. I went back to "the trestle" years later and marveled that such a place ever held our "white water" rafting trips, our timeless afternoons when the whole world stood still. But through a city-child's eyes, it was an oasis. 'Round the back of a fence, down a hill, and we could leave the rush of the city behind us. Our capacity for play made it so.

When I watch my children meet the world each day, I realize new meaning in "discovery," "fascination," "enthusiasm." I hear their awe-filled murmurings, and I know there is much I do not see, touch, taste, rub up against. . . . Can I learn to pause in my reaching ahead? Can I become an explorer of this time and place? Play is the ability to throw oneself fully and joyfully into the present moment. When we play, we release memory and yearning. We find that the moment at hand is sufficient to hold us, and we wallow in it like a sparkling river on a hot summer day. As I play with my children, I am reminded: I cannot choose now or tomorrow. I can only choose to see or not to see this world unfolding before my eyes.

Simple Rituals to Celebrate Play

Circle Around

Create a "circle time" each day for 10 to 20 minutes where you can enjoy singing, rhyming, and movement. Use singing games, songs, and verses that will adapt themselves well to simple gestures. Singing and speaking familiar verses stimulates a child's memory, such an important element of early childhood development. If you have a baby, create an intimate "circle time," using such verses as "Pat-a-Cake" and "This Little Piggy." For children 2-5, circle games like "A-Ring Around o' Roses" provide a sense of belonging and security. Children from 5-8 will thrive on more complex circle games, and children 9 and up will thrive on line and spiral games with a group of friends. These games for older children reflect the need for a growing independence and "going on a journey in the world."

It's Raining, It's Pouring

On rainy days, go to the window with your child and observe the character of the rain: Is it a gentle rain or a stormy gale? Does it look as if it will rain all day or only drizzle for a short while? And most importantly, ask, "What does the rain bring?" Perhaps it brings blossoms on the trees or daffodils springing up. Perhaps it brings a cleaner street or the melting of snow. Or perhaps . . . the rain brings the "rain toys." Transform a toy chest, old suitcase, or cardboard box into a treasure chest of fun. Add musical instruments, toys, costumes, or craft projects. You might want to rotate the contents from time to time. A new puzzle or book might also be a cherished addition. You may want to keep your rainy day surprises in a special place, hide them in a new place each time they are used, or create a treasure hunt, using the "rain toys" as the "pot of gold."

Moving On

When you need to complete a particular activity or guide your child in a new direction, use a song or verse that will signal the change. Fantasy is a helpful tool. When our children hedged climbing the stairs to their rooms for naptime and bedtime, we imagined the stairs as a big mountain to climb, and from this game the song "Climbin' Up the Mountain" (page 73) came forth. It was a simple key to their cooperation and more pleasant for all of us. A preschool teacher I know gathers the children in his class by becoming a "conductor," asking all to "get aboard" the train. Consider using such songs as "Come to the Circle" (page 70) or "Follow, Follow Me" (page 71) to signal a change of activities.

Letting Go

Since toys carry a place of honor in the lives of children, it can be a meaningful experience to acknowledge the departure of an old toy. Allowing a child to say goodbye to a toy that is worn or being passed on can be a significant tool for the child to feel the completion of a relationship with the toy. Perhaps the child can draw a picture as a special remembrance or write a poem about it. In the past, when we have donated toys to charities, I have imagined with my children the faces of the young folks who would find joy in our giving. There are many opportunities when a loss may be transformed. One of my fondest memories as a child was the day I dropped a cherished "piggy bank" my oldest brother had given me, and it shattered into a thousand pieces. Hours later, my brother appeared, coming from the house of the "piggy bank fairy," so he said. He handed me a bank that was the same color and size as the one I had broken, but this one was sitting in a different position . . . " the piggy bank fairy didn't get it quite right when she put it back together again," so my brother explained. I was filled with awe and wonder, and I marveled that my brother should have such impressive connections.

Living Stories

Artistic tools can be an inspiration for a child to express the gifts of imagination. In the Waldorf classroom a story is told while the children warm beeswax in their hands. When it is pliable, they begin to shape the characters of the story while they are listening. The story begins to live in them through these creations. If you do not have beeswax handy, try using modeling clay or homemade Play-Doh, which can be kneaded using 3 parts flour, 1 part salt, and 1 part water. After the "characters" are shaped, set them in a special place where you and your child can enjoy them.

Natural Wonders

My children and I enjoy taking walks together. As we walk, we keep our eyes open for gifts of nature: feathers, unusual rocks, an abandoned bird's nest, a broken bird shell, colorful leaves that have fallen, seed pods, fallen branches, an empty cocoon. . . . We create a "nature table" in a corner of our home where we can display these treasures. A display table can be made easily by finding a sturdy box and draping it with a cloth, or you may wish to use the center of your dining room table for these special findings. When you add new items to your "gifts from nature," consider holding hands around the nature table and singing a song of thanks and praise for these gifts. For a nature table blessing, you may want to use the second verse of "For the Beauty of the Earth" (page 54).

Passageways for Parents: Play

Playful, inviting settings draw children to interact with their environment. Look around your house and your child's room and discover corners you can transform into playful settings. Younger children will be prompted by a child-sized kitchen with stove and sink, pots and pans, and a child-sized broom. One family I know made a stove by painting burners on an old white table and hanging curtains around it to create a cabinet area underneath. An old basin could work well as a sink. Other playful settings for young ones might include: an arts and crafts table, a quiet storybook corner, a dress-up corner with clothes hooks or a hall tree for costumes, or a puppet corner. Display toys in a way that is pleasing to the eye and imagination. Little dolls or gnomes gathered around a table for tea may prompt your child to play out a story of a tea party. Toys displayed on a bookshelf will be played with far more often than those stuffed away in a toy box. For older children, consider a workbench and tools for woodworking; a craft corner with materials for favorite crafts; a display table for a rock, shell, coin, or stamp collection; or a reading corner.

Selecting, making, and caring for toys requires a reverent awareness and can be a ritual in itself. The toys we select for and with our children reflect the quality of our lives. Some of the old-fashioned toys will enhance a child's creativity and imagination far more than the most intricate new toys on the market. Consider jump ropes; rag dolls; cardboard puzzles; cardboard boxes; natural blocks cut from various sized wooden logs; toys made of natural, unvarnished wood, cotton, wool, etc. Use natural baskets for doll cradles, bean bags, building blocks, and seashells. Use cotton bags for rock collections, jacks, and marbles. It took our family two years, many talks with well-meaning relatives, and several trips to charity drop-offs to make the transition to more natural toys, and still we have a few "stragglers." If you feel you need to make changes in this area, a gentle transition is preferable.

Your child's play will be further enhanced if you give time for uninterrupted free-play to allow your child's imagination room to roam. Try not to interject conversation and put demands on your child during these interludes. As you watch your child, you will discover natural pauses in their play that are appropriate transition moments in which you can guide your child toward clean-up time or some other activity in the day.

There are times, of course, when *you* will be your child's most cherished playmate. Remember to take time to genuinely play with your child. Share spontaneous laughter, silliness, mischievous adventure. When was the last time you rolled down a hill, flew a kite, had a tickle hug? When was the last time you climbed a tree, played hide-and-seek, pretended to be a wizard or a ballet dancer? Throw inhibition to the wind and let the child inside you out for an excursion.

▶ Flutterby

Hand Movements for "Flutterby"

Start with hands crossed, palms facing you. Hook thumbs to create butterfly.

Don't flutter by butterfly,

Start butterfly in front of chest. Flap wings out and away to the right.

Come rest on my finger,

Make fist with left hand, extend pointer finger. Lay right palm on pointer. Flap right fingers up and down.

Come tickle my cheek,

Flap right fingers lightly against right cheek.

Come be my guest for the day
    or the week,

Left palm up in front of chest, start with right hand out and up to the right. Flap right fingers and bring them slowly to hover over left palm.

But don't flutter . . .

Still flapping fingers, move right hand out and up to right again.

'Bye, butterfly.

Transform flapping fingers into a wave "good-bye."

▶ Come-a-runnin'

"Come-a, come-a-runnin',
come-a-runnin' when I call,"
said the afternoon sun in its quiet sort of way,
"for the river needs a-splashin' in,
the meadow needs a-rollin' in,
and I need the laughter of your play."

"Come-a, come-a-runnin',
come-a-runnin' when I call,
come and wind your way through my threads of gold.
Weave your greatest pleasure,
from an afternoon of leisure.
My children, come-a-runnin', young and old."

▶ Two Little Spiders[*]

Two little spiders
  hanging in the air,
Said one to the other,
  "Shall we play here or there?
Shall we climb up
  someone's leg?
Shall we hide in
  someone's hair?"
When you're a little spider,
  you can play 'most anywhere.
Said the other little spider,
  "My dear friend, please beware.
There are giants who roam about,
  whom our little bodies scare."
And then (clap!) . . .
those little spiders
  disappeared in thin air,
for a giant who roams about
  "did in" the little pair . . .
Those playful little spiders,
  unfortunate little spiders,
those playful little spiders
  who were hanging in the air.

Hand Movements for "Two Little Spiders"

Begin with both hands dangling above head.

Raise right hand slightly and move fingers.

Swoop right hand down and then up in a straight line to starting position.

Circle right hand above own head.

Raise left hand slightly above right and move fingers.

Clap, holding hands together.

Show disappointment on your face

Open up palms to look at "the spiders" sadly.

Raise hands again with two "spiders" dangling above head.

* With children six and under, it is best not to use a great deal of drama when relaying a story, especially if it includes images the child may find scary or sad. Death and sadness are a part of life, and just as they should not be ignored, neither should they be overly stressed. In this way children may absorb the images in their own way, without the images being thrust upon them.

◗ *An Apple a Day* (Rhythm Game)

(Person/group 1 begins; then 2nd person/group joins in. Pick up the tempo a bit as you repeat.)

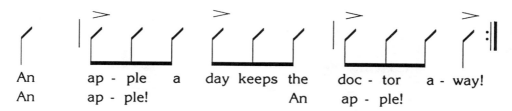

An   ap - ple a day keeps the   doc - tor a - way!
An   ap - ple!   An ap - ple!

◗ *Bushel of Blueberries*

We brought a bushel of blueberries
back from the patch,
Mama jellied and canned a batch,
Daddy made a blueberry pie,
Me and Sis, well, I can't lie,
With the berries, the pie, the home-made jellies . . .
We ended up with blueberry bellies.

◗ *Three Gray Geese* (Rhythm Game)

(Person/group 1 begins, to establish the rhythm. The part for person/group 2 is in parentheses.
First add the "honks" at the end of each sentence; then add the "honks" in the middle.)

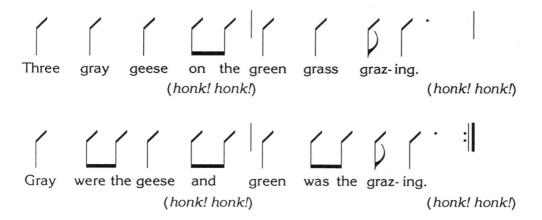

Three   gray   geese   on the green grass graz- ing.
          (*honk! honk!*)   (*honk! honk!*)

Gray   were the geese and   green was the graz- ing.
          (*honk! honk!*)   (*honk! honk!*)

Songs for Play

Come to the Circle

Gently

Shea Darian

Come to the cir - cle where dreams are found,

Take my hand, we'll dance a - round: Ha-

la, Ha - la, Ha - la, Ha - lo,

Round and round and round we go.

Follow, Follow Me

Brightly

Shea Darian

Fol - low, fol - low me to the ring of the fair - ies,

Fol - low, fol - low me where the fair - ies dance and sing.

Gath - er with me here all the mag - ic you can car - ry as we

cir - cle and cir - cle 'round the danc - ing fair - y ring.

*Could strum a "G" chord throughout.

Grasshoppers Three

3-part round

Folksong

Grass - hop - pers three a - fid - dl - ing went,
Hey, ho, ne - ver be still! They
paid no mon - ey to - ward their rent, but
all day long with el - bow bent They
fid - dled a tune called Ril - la - by - ril - la - by,
Fid - dled a tune called Ril - la - by rill.

Climbin' Up the Mountain

Moderately

Shea Darian

1. Climb - in' up the moun - tain, climb-in' so—— high,
2. Climb - in' up the moun - tain, made it to the top,
3. Climb - in' down the moun - tain, climb-in' so—— low,

Climb - in' up the moun - tain to the——— sky,
Climb - in' up the moun - tain, we did not stop,
Climb - in' down the moun - tain, a - way we go,

One step, two steps, three steps, four,
One step, two steps, three steps, four,
One step, two steps, three steps, four,

Five steps, six steps, then we climb some more.
Five steps, six steps, then we climbed some more.
Five steps, six steps, 'till we reach the floor.

*Could strum a "G" chord throughout.

A Ram Sam Sam

2-part round

Moroccan Folksong

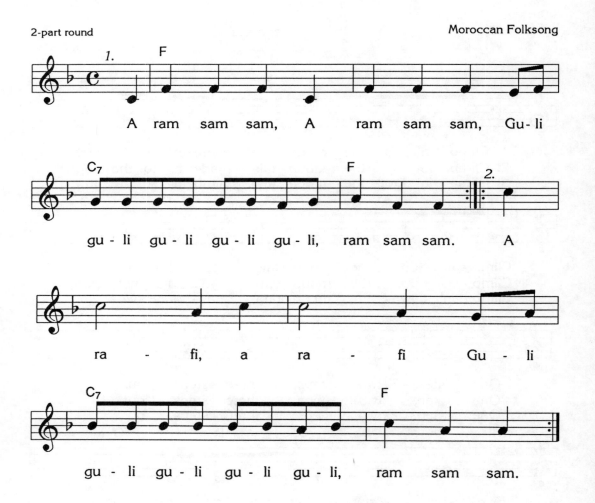

A ram sam sam, A ram sam sam, Gu-li
gu - li gu - li gu - li gu - li, ram sam sam. A
ra - fi, a ra - fi Gu - li
gu - li gu - li gu - li gu - li, ram sam sam.

Let Us Sing Together

4-part round

Czechoslovakian Folksong

Let us sing to-geth-er, Let us sing to-geth-er, One and all a joy - ous song.

Let us sing to - geth - er, One and all a joy - ous song.

Let us sing a - gain and a-gain, Let us sing a-gain and a-gain,

Let us sing a - gain and a-gain, One and all a joy - ous song.

Stories for Play

William's Doll by *Charlotte Zolotow*   (3 - 8)

William wants a doll more than anything in the world. His parents try to appease him with more masculine interests. William's brother and his friend tease him for being a sissy. Finally, William's grandmother is the one who understands the importance of a child having a doll to nurture and hold. (New York: HarperCollins Children's Books, 1972)

The First Song Ever Sung by *Laura Krauss Melmed*   (3 - 9)

A boy asks, "What was the first song ever sung?" The boy's family members, as well as the minnows and the birds, answer the question out of their own experience. The artwork is dreamy and exquisite. (New York: Lothrop, Lee, & Shepard, 1993)

The Whale's Song by *Dyan Sheldon*   (3 - 9)

Lilly's grandmother tells stories of the whales she knew as a child. She tells how she befriended the whales, and how once or twice she heard them sing. Lilly is taken with her grandmother's memories and imagines the whales by night and day. Finally, the whales come to Lilly beneath a starlit sky. The paintings by Gary Blythe are sensitive and exceptional. (New York: Dial Books for Young Readers, 1990)

Amazing Grace by *Mary Hoffman*   (4 - 10)

Grace's favorite pastime is dressing in home-made costumes and imagining herself as a spider, a doctor, or whatever else her imagination holds. When she and her classmates have a chance to audition for their class play, "Peter Pan," Grace wishes to be Peter, but is told by classmates that a "black" girl could never play the role of Peter. With support from her mother and grandmother, Grace surprises everyone. (New York: Dial Books for Young Readers, 1991)

Roxaboxen by *Alice McLerran*   (4 - 10)

A true story about a group of children who create their own city at the edge of town. This delightful book illustrates the power of imagination and play in the lives of children. (New York: Puffin Books, 1991)

Cornrows by *Camille Yarbrough*   (4 -12)

Shirley Ann tells of the playful singing and storytelling that goes on each day as her mother and grandmother braid cornrows in the children's hair and tell of their African heritage and the tradition of cornrowed hair. The children are enthralled with the game that follows the braiding — to name the cornrow style on their heads. Play transforms a history lesson into an afternoon of fun. (New York: Putnam Publishing Group, 1981)

A Playtime Tale to Spin

"Mr. Korbis"

Hen and Rooster lived out in the country, and one day decided they would visit their neighbor a few miles down the road. So they made a sturdy carriage, with four magnificent red wheels on it. Proudly, they showed the carriage to their four friends, the field mice, and asked if the mice would draw the carriage on the journey. When the mice obliged, Rooster and Hen harnessed them to the carriage and climbed up inside. Away they went, and you could see those red wheels comin' for quite a distance.

Along the way, they met Cat on the edge of the road, who waved them to a stop and called out, "Where are you going?" Rooster and Hen sang out:

> *"Whatever may be,*
> *we're off to see*
> *our neighbor Mr. Korbis."*

"May I come with you?" Cat asked.

"Of course," answered Rooster, "climb up and join us."

Along the way, Hen and Rooster sang, and soon Cat joined in:

> *"Be careful not to dirty*
> *our wheels that turn about,*
> *Little carriage, roll on,*
> *Little mice, pipe out,*
> *Whatever may be,*
> *We're off to see*
> *our neighbor Mr. Korbis."*

The travelers met others along the road who joined them: a Duck, an Egg, a Pin, a Needle, and a Millstone. They sang happily as they rode along:

> *"Be careful not to dirty*
> *our wheels that turn about,*
> *Little carriage, roll on,*
> *Little mice, pipe out,*

Whatever may be,
We're off to see
our neighbor Mr. Korbis."

Finally, they arrived at Mr. Korbis' house. They knocked and called, but Mr. Korbis was nowhere to be seen. So Rooster and Hen perched themselves to wait. The mice ran off to Mr. Korbis' barn to store the carriage. Cat curled up by Mr. Korbis' fireplace. Duck settled in by Mr. Korbis' well. Egg rolled itself up in Mr. Korbis' towel. Pin found a comfortable place in Mr. Korbis' easy chair. Needle lay itself to rest in Mr. Korbis' bed pillow. And Millstone set itself on a ledge over Mr. Korbis' doorway. They all had a peaceful rest, until Mr. Korbis came home.

Mr. Korbis went straight to the fireplace to stoke up a fire for his dinner, but Cat woke up scared and threw ashes right in Mr. Korbis' face. He hurried off to the well to clean himself up, but Duck spit water right in Mr. Korbis' eyes. He ran for a towel to wipe himself, but Egg splattered and stuck Mr. Korbis' eyes shut.

Mr. Korbis was so upset from all this flurry, he flopped into his easy chair. "Ouch!" Pin stuck him good. Mr. Korbis flung himself onto his bed, thinking he could surely find rest there, but when he lay on his pillow, Needle stuck him hard. He jumped up and found his way outside to the barn, thinking he'd hop on his horse and ride away. But as he opened the door to the barn, the mice skittered out and up his legs. Mr. Korbis ran about the yard, kicking at the mice. He made his way toward his house to get away from the little creatures, but just as he found the doorway, Millstone jumped down and knocked him out cold. Just then, Hen and Rooster woke from their perch, saw Mr. Korbis stretched out in the doorway, and sang out:

"Whatever may be,
We've come to see
our neighbor Mr. Korbis!"

(A Grimms' tale, retold by Shea Darian)

If you question the "playfulness" of this tale, tell it to a kindergarten or first grade child a few times, and I think you'll be convinced. Sometimes we need our children to lead us toward the playful humor of life.

4 ▶ Working Wonders

Celebrating Work

> "Work is love made visible.
> And if you cannot work with love but only with distaste,
> it is better that you should leave your work
> and sit at the gate of the temple
> and take alms of those who work with joy."
>
> — Kahlil Gibran

Celebrating Work

Years ago my mother told me she would have been eternally satisfied being a homemaker and parent. She said her years at home, raising children, were deeply rewarding. When I heard this, I puzzled at the thought of anyone (especially my mother, the gifted woman) envisioning the rewards in her life in such simple terms. Now I know better, as I meet the daily demands of parenthood.

Chop wood. Carry water. Wash dishes. Sweep floors. Bake bread. Wipe noses. Mow grass. Pick up toys. Fold clothes. Small gestures of usefulness. Small gestures. Small. As I wash dishes, I look at my hands and smile at how much they are becoming replicas of my mother's. I see her ironing freshly laundered clothes, slicing bread from the oven, tying the laces of my shoes. Her hands moved from task to task, as if they were opening intimately to the mystery of the ordinary.

Some days I forget the mystery. I grudge bringing the vacuum from the closet and am inspired to enlist the assistance of two four-year-old friends, who happen to be playing in my living room. I sit cross-legged on the couch and watch their efforts intently. First, they grasp the clumsy beast together, their bodies swooping back and forth to a rhythm only they can understand. One of them becomes tired, sits to rest, watches the other at work. The vacuum switches hands eight or nine times before the job is finished. They both look up at me as if I have given them a shiny new bicycle. I will never vacuum my rugs the same again. The four-year-olds have converted me.

With these everyday hands, we birth usefulness and purpose. We create a compassionate servitude that can only be wrought through ordinary actions. When I see Andrew finish washing and folding a mountain of laundry and stack it neatly in our drawers, his work holds more promise than a love letter. When Willa rinses and stacks the dishes, or Morgan sweeps the kitchen floor, I feel our home and family is esteemed through the purpose in their fingertips.

These days as I watch my hands opening more intimately to such small endeavors, I think of my mother hundreds of miles away, and I whisper, "No greater gift could you bestow." Chop wood. Carry water. "Work is love made visible." Our children will see it and sense it through the joy and meaning we find in our daily tasks. And they will be nurtured through these small gestures of compassion . . . for the way we come to small things shows our reverence for all things.

Simple Rituals to Celebrate Work

Pick-up Quick

After playtime, when toys are scattered, create a cleanup ritual with your child. In this way the child can experience the rhythm of taking apart and putting back together again. Energetic songs and verses will go a long way for this one. When putting blocks back in the block basket, "One potato, two potato" may keep little hands working. Remember Mary Poppins' "spoon full of sugar"? I will vouch for its magic.

Fresh from the Oven

Baking bread with your child can be a cherished weekly ritual. Children enjoy foods they have made by the work of their own hands. When you bake bread at home, make an extra loaf for a friend or neighbor. Older children can deliver it themselves.

A Room a Day

Sometimes it is difficult to balance housework with the other needs of family life. The family who thrives on organization may wish to set aside a time each day to clean and organize one area of the house. Perhaps Monday is the living/dining room, Tuesday is the kitchen, Wednesday the bathroom, etc. . . . Or you may wish to divide the rooms of your house among you for one month. At the end of the day, each family member can go to their appointed room and tidy it up. When cleaning, remember not to leave toddlers out of the picture. They will thrive on such small tasks as moving onions and potatoes one by one from one bowl to another. Their work may not seem significant to the cleaning of the kitchen (and may cause you to sweep one more time), but this kind of parallel activity will free you to accomplish much and allow your child to enjoy the work of toddlerhood.

Swarming

I know one family with four children who uses a cleaning ritual especially appropriate when it is necessary to straighten up quickly. The whole family goes into one room together and names the tasks that need to be done. Then, like bees, they "swarm" the room until all the tasks are completed. Sometimes they guess how long it will take them to tidy a room. They set a timer and try to "beat the clock." Try it!

Uncluttering

At the end of each year, your family may want to have an "uncluttering" ritual when you recycle or give away clothes you have outgrown, items you no longer use, or spares you have accumulated. Think of friends and acquaintances to whom these items would be useful, donate them to a charity, or take them to a consignment shop. A few years ago, we had all of our possessions stolen from public storage while we were waiting to move into our new home. It was a rude awakening, but we suddenly realized how few of our possessions were necessary or significant to us.

Needles and Pins

Some of the most rewarding work can be discovered in the traditional hand-crafts: knitting, crocheting, basketweaving, woodworking, needlepoint, hand sewing. . . . Choose a craft project to make and give away as gifts. What a joy for children to learn the intricacies of a craft and have the opportunity to share the useful and beautiful objects made from their own hands. If you do not know any hand-crafts, there is sure to be a craftsperson nearby who would be willing to teach you. Grandparents are usually thrilled when someone values their craft, and they are delighted to pass it on. If you do not know any craftspeople, consider venturing to a retirement community where crafts often abound and your companionship would be deeply appreciated.

How Do They Do It?

Talk as a family about the occupations that arouse your curiosity. Choose a special day once a month and seek out opportunities to observe the work of an old-time blacksmith, woodcarver, potter, pizzamaker, astronomer, dancer, violinist, painter, cartoonist, garbage collector, cement layer, bookbinder, or whomever you desire to know more about. Your family can develop an appreciation and understanding for a wide variety of workers and their work.

Pitching In

Be aware of people you know who are in need of assistance: families who may be moving to a new home, someone with a new baby, someone who has experienced the death of a loved one, someone who needs to find food or shelter, someone experiencing a divorce or broken relationship, etc. . . . Gather as a family to meditate upon friends you know who are in need and consider their circumstances. Each family member may want to offer a prayer or wish for these friends. Then think of ways your family can work to help. Sometimes even a few hours of assistance is a great help.

Passageways for Parents: Work

Since young children learn through imitation, one of the most significant gifts we may share with them is a love and appreciation for the work of our own hands. I used to wonder why Morgan and Willa seemed more satisfied playing alongside Andrew's activities than mine, even though I interacted and played with them more. I finally realized it was due to the fact that children thrive on the household activities and rhythmic movements of their caregivers. Andrew has a natural ability to accomplish daily household tasks, while keeping an eye and ear peeled for the children's occasional needs — a skill I had to learn.

From the time your child is three, ask yourself what simple household chores your child is able to fulfill, such as setting the napkins or silverware around the table at mealtime. As your child matures, consider greater responsibilities that correlate with your child's capabilities. Observe your child at specific tasks and ask, "What jobs are not too difficult but enough of a challenge for my child to make the task interesting?" If your child is too young to carry out a task alone, how might you encourage their interest in the work? If you put an old sock on the hand of an eighteen-month-old, they are sure to pick up *some* of the dust on the table top or piano bench. If a preschooler shows interest in the bookshelf you are building, you might let them hand you the nails, or set them up with a wooden carpenter's set. Young children are thrilled to receive a child-sized version of a working tool. A little person's broom, rake, work gloves, hammer, or screwdriver can assist your child in making valuable contributions. You might purchase a reel lawn mower for an older child to cut the lawn.

One way to help your child be aware of seasonal cycles is through work specific to each season. Planting seedlings for a garden in the spring; mowing grass in the summer; raking in the fall; keeping the bird feeder filled in the winter. As we interact with the cycles of nature, we observe these changes with a keener eye.

Remember to praise your child for a job well done. Gently point out ways your child can improve on a task. Most of us underestimate the work power of our children. The secret of guiding children toward an appreciation for their work-ability is to foster the natural joy for work that children bring into this world.

Verses for Work

▶ *To Meet a Task*

I meet my work
with strong limbs,
open hands,
proud heart.

(with fists, raise arms out in front, chest height)

(open hands with palms up)

(cross hands and bring palms to chest)

▶ *There Was an Old Woman*

There was an old woman tossed in a blanket,
Seventeen times as high as the moon;
But where she was going, no mortal could tell,
For under her arm she carried a broom.
Old woman, old woman, old woman, said I,
Whither, ah whither, ah whither so high?
To sweep the cobwebs from the sky,
And I'll be with you by and by.
      — Anonymous

▶ *Working Hands*

Sometimes I have to set my mind a-right,
     and my heart too,
If I want my hands to do the things
     I'm asking them to do.

▶ *Song of the Sky Loom*

O our Mother the Earth, O our Father the Sky,
Your children are we, and with tired backs
We bring you gifts.
     — Tewa North American Indians

▶ Life Sculpture

Chisel in hand stood a sculptor boy
      With his marble block before him,
And his eyes lit up with a smile of joy,
      As an angel-dream passed o'er him.

He carved the dream on that shapeless stone,
      With many a sharp incision;
With heaven's own light the sculpture shone,
      He'd caught that angel-vision.

                — George Washington Doane

▶ When Work Is Done

There is a pause when work is done,
A blessing for the task completed:
I rejoice in the strength of my bones
who welcomed labor as a guest.

Songs for Work

I Will Work with Joy

Brightly   Shea Darian

I will work with joy, my task is now be-gun,

I will work with joy un-til my task is done. Per-

sist-ence and pride, pur-pose un-folds, as

I work hard to reach my goals.

A Place for Everything

Words adapted from
Isabella Mary Beeton

Shea Darian

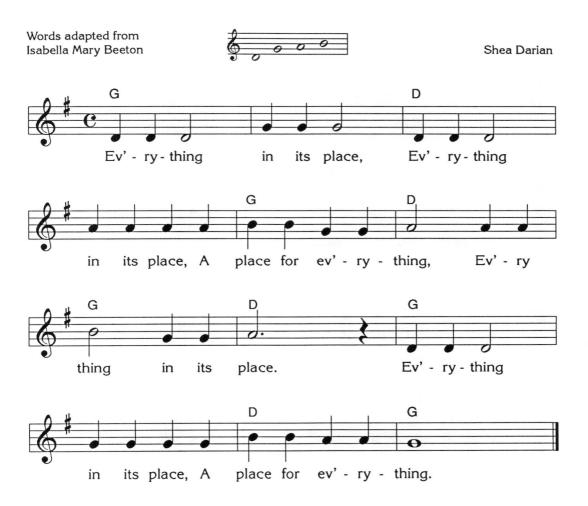

A place for everything and everything in its place.
— Isabella Mary Beeton

The Blacksmith

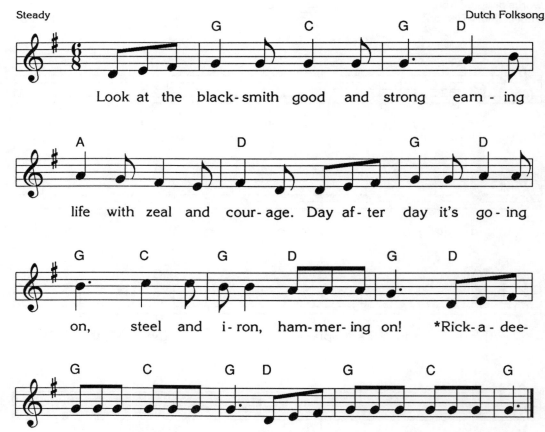

Steady   Dutch Folksong

Look at the black-smith good and strong earn-ing

life with zeal and cour-age. Day af-ter day it's go-ing

on, steel and i-ron, ham-mer-ing on! *Rick-a-dee-

rack-a-dee, rick-a-dee rack! Rick-a-dee-rack-a-dee, rick-a-dee rack!

*Actions:
On "Rickadee-rackadee" section, make fists and hammer right fist on left, then left fist on right.

Work-a-day

3-part round

Shea Darian

We are a-ble, we are strong, We work well as we

sing this song: Work-a-day, work-a-day, one and all, When

work is done, we stand tall, Work-a-day, work-a-day,

one and all, When work is done, we stand tall.

Hot, Brown Loaf

Purposefully

Shea Darian

We mix the dough, we knead the dough, We let it

rise, We punch the dough and pat the dough. It

grows be-fore our eyes. Hot, brown loaf from a lit-tle

ball, It ris - es up to feed us all.

Many Hands

3-part round*
Words adapted from
John Heywood

Shea Darian

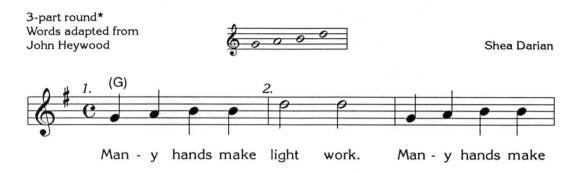

Man - y hands make light work. Man - y hands make

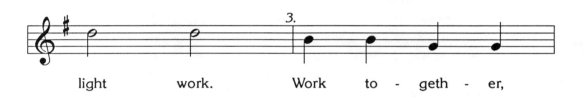

light work. Work to - geth - er,

work to - geth - er, man - y hands.

Many hands make light work.
— John Heywood

*Although rounds are more appropriate for older elementary children, this song may be used as a unison melody for younger children.

Stories for Work

Frederick by Leo Lionni (3 - 9)

While all the other mice in the mouse family are working hard gathering food for winter, Frederick is busy gathering colors and sunshine and words. The other mice discover that Frederick's type of work is honorable and valuable as well. (New York: Pantheon, 1967)

The Legend of Indian Paintbrush by Tomie de Paola (3 - 10)

A young Indian boy has a dream vision that one day he will paint the colors of the evening sky. He learns to follow his gifts, even though it means doing work that is different from the other boys in the tribe. (New York: G.P. Putnam's Sons, 1988)

Keep the Lights Burning, Abbie by Peter and Connie Roop (4 - 12)

A true story of Abbie Burgess, whose father was a lighthouse keeper off the coast of Maine in 1853. He leaves Abbie in charge of the lighthouse when he goes to the mainland for supplies and medicine for Abbie's sick mother. A storm rages. Abbie's father is unable to return for four weeks. The story reveals Abbie's fears, conviction, and courage as she keeps the lights burning, and as she and her sisters care for their home and their mother. (Minneapolis: Carolrhoda Books, 1985)

When Clay Sings by Byrd Baylor (5 -12)

A celebration of ancient pottery made by Indians of the Southwest. Reveals the sacred qualities of this "slow and gentle work. No hurrying. No rushing." (New York: Macmillan Children's Book Group, 1987)

The Canada Geese Quilt by Natalie Kinsey-Warnock (8 - 12)

Ten-year-old Ariel struggles with the thought of her parents having a new baby. But Grandma prompts her to help in making a quilt for the arrival, which they work on together. Then Grandma suffers a stroke, and Ariel must find the will to finish the quilt herself. A sensitive family story that will bring laughter and tears. (South Holland, IL: Dell Publishers, 1989)

Sugaring Time by Kathryn Lasky (8 - 12)

Vivid photographs follow a family's work as they gather sap in the maple grove and boil it into maple syrup. Strong images of parents and children working side by side. (New York: Macmillan Children's Book Group, 1983)

"The Mouse, the Bird, and the Sausage"

Once upon a time there lived together three friends: a mouse, a bird, and a sausage. They lived together with happy hearts, for they had learned to work side-by-side. Each one had their own special work to do, and each one did it well. The mouse carried the water, made the fire, and set the table. The sausage was the cook. And the bird flew to the forest to gather firewood for the following day.

One day, as the bird searched for wood, he came upon another bird and began to sing the praises of his life with the mouse and the sausage. The other bird began to tease him, saying: "What a fool you are! You are the one doing all the work. You must come to the forest every day and gather wood, while your friends stay home, doing close to nothing."

On the way home, the bird thought about what the other bird had said. It was true each day after the mouse carried the water and made the fire, she rested in her room until the sausage called her to set the table. And the sausage simply had to sit by the soup pot, make sure that it was boiling, and in the end, wriggle through the pot once or twice to spice up the food. The bird arrived home with the firewood to find the mouse and sausage, as usual, sitting at the table, ready to eat. After they finished eating, they slept with full bellies and happy hearts.

But the next morning when they awoke, the bird said to his friends: "I will not go to the forest to gather wood today. You have tricked me long enough. I am not your slave or your fool! I will stay right here and do your work, while one of you makes the trip to the forest."

The sausage and the mouse argued and argued with the bird, but as the day passed and no dinner was in the making, the two gave in and said they would try the bird's new plan. The three friends agreed to draw lots, and in this way it was decided that the bird had to carry water, build the fire, and set the table; the mouse would do the cooking; and the sausage must be the one to gather firewood in the forest.

Well, you must be wondering how the new plan turned out. The sausage went out into the forest. The bird made the fire so the mouse could put the pot on, and then they waited for the sausage to return with the firewood. But the sausage did not return, and they were so worried that the bird went to find out what had happened. Not far from their home, the bird met a dog who had swallowed the sausage for a tasty dinner. The bird was furious, but the dog claimed the sausage was fair game.

Sadly, the bird returned home to tell the mouse. They grieved over the loss of their friend but were determined to stick together and make the best of it. The bird set the table, and the mouse went on cooking. Just before the soup was done, the mouse thought she would wriggle through the pot, as she had seen the sausage do. She hopped in but could not hop out, for that boiling pot was no place for a mouse! It took her and cooked her.

When the bird went to set the meal on the table, the mouse was not there. The bird searched and called out for his friend, but she was nowhere to be seen or heard. The bird walked about in a daze, and careless as he was, his tailfeathers caught fire. The bird hurried to the well for water to put the fire out, but just as he reached the well, the bucket slipped. The bird fell in after it. So, in the end, that poor, careless bird was drowned.

(A Grimms' tale, retold by Shea Darian)

5 ▶ Listen to the Quiet
Celebrating Quiet

'I have seen
A curious child, who dwelt upon a tract
Of inland ground, applying to his ear
The convolutions of a smooth-lipped shell,
To which, in silence hushed, his very soul
Listened intensely . . .'

— William Wordsworth

Celebrating Quiet

A few summers ago, my sister gave me a glistening spiral seashell. "They say that if you hold a shell to your ear, you will hear the ocean," she wrote to me. "I think, rather, that in quiet listening, you hear the whisperings of your spirit." Words from one who has ears in her eyes and feet and fingers. When we were children, she was "reserved," the "quiet one." In truth, she was the one always listening, not so much to sound as to all that was not sound.

In quiet listening we penetrate a depth of truth that can renew our souls. The subtleties of nature vibrate with ancient wisdom. If we are silent enough to hear the invitation, we are welcomed as humble participants into the most tender movements of creation.

Lying in bed with Willa. She is yelling, wiggling, kicking. She does not want to sleep. Does not want to leave this world for a moment. I hold her in my arms, coo to her, sing to her, become silent with her. She drifts with heavy eyes, open mouth, one last huge sigh. Her rosy-cheeked breath is faster than my own. I suspend myself in the quietness of our breathing.

How many of us come to quiet moments as a child fighting sleep? Reluctant to release the world of sound. Non-stop conversation, the TV, the radio, the Walkman . . . What are we trying to drown with all this noise? The alternative must be frightening to us: to hear each other, our own spirit, and silence, unknown silence.

As a child, I stood beside the railroad tracks that bordered the back of our two-acre lot. Caught up by the motion and sound of the rushing train. The magnificent steel turning, shifting, rumbling in the earth beneath my bare feet. Then bursting out of my child-play, vanishing on its way. I would sit in the grass and let the silence grow inside me. Let the quiet hold me. For in the quiet, the grass, the trees, the ants, the dirt would whisper to me. At least that is when I could hear them.

Silence is a wise sage who brings us knowledge to which our ears are deaf. The languages of creation are many and varied. We may hear them if we listen. Listen with our "very souls."

And so, led by the wisdom of our children, we turn to the whispering grass and talking trees. We clear a path for quiet. For if we have not paused with our children in silence this day, how will we know we are truly alive? How will we know, unless we have heard one another's breath and heartbeat?

Simple Rituals to Celebrate Quiet

A Pause a Day

Create a quiet time each day when your child can nap or partake in a quiet activity. Begin nap or quiet time with a song, verse, or story. For a younger child who no longer takes naps, quiet time might consist of looking through a stack of picture books or the family photo albums. Even older children need a time of silent relaxation each day — if not for resting, then perhaps for reading or taking a warm bath. Individual quiet time might also be inspired by repetitive crafts or simple tasks that can help clear a buzzing mind. Finger-knitting, weaving a basket, or beading a necklace can bathe one in silent relaxation. A young child may produce this same kind of focused energy through such tasks as carding wool fleece, stringing large wooden beads, or separating marbles or beads by color into individual bowls. End your child's quiet time with a bell, chime, or quiet song.

Read the Signs

Learn some sign language with your child and set aside a time each day when you speak with one another only through signs. Speaking through signs and gestures can produce a more focused way of communicating and can help us not only penetrate the wall that often hinders communication between hearing and deaf persons, but also open up our awareness of the human need to be understood in ways that reach beyond verbal communication.

Open Your Ears

Whenever things get especially noisy, play a listening game in which someone calls, "Open your ears!" Sit in silence for a minute and listen to the sounds around you. After the silence, name the sounds you heard. If there is an unidentified sound, follow it to its source. Play this game with a child who is frightened of things that "go bump in the night." Uncover the creaks and thuds that produce goblins in the dark.

Silent Meditations

Guide your child into silent moments, perhaps at the same time each day. A few minutes of shared quiet will help you see each other more clearly and sensitively — and can save you an hour or two of chaos. If you have created a prayer corner in your home, you may want to use it for these quiet interludes. It might be helpful to light a candle and gaze at the flame; or create a tone to begin and end the silence by tapping a spoon on the rim of a glass, blowing over the top of a partially filled juice or pop bottle, or ringing finger cymbals. Let the tone lead you and your child into the center of silence and then invite you back into the world of sound with greater awareness. You may want to try a simple breathing exercise together. Sit cross-legged facing each other and notice one another's breathing until you are inhaling and exhaling at the same time. Or hold your palms up a few inches away from your child's palms; inhale as your child exhales, exhale as your child inhales. You may want to close your quiet time with a verse and grounding gesture, such as crossing the forearms and placing one's palms on the chest. This sort of quiet pause is especially helpful when you or your child is hassled or distressed in some way. Afterward, you and your child will be more able to meet the needs before you.

Walking on the Wild Side

Take silent walks around your neighborhood and become aware of the wildlife that surrounds you; or find a forest trail or a patch of the country where you can hike. Along the way, find a comfortable place where you can sit in silence and listen to the sounds of nature. In *Sharing Nature with Children* (listed in the "Great Books for Parents" section of the Appendices, page 207), Joseph Cornell suggests sitting with nature long enough so that you become part of it. Animals will come closer, the human eye will become more accustomed to the intricacies of wildlife. After your experience, talk with your child about what you have seen and heard.

Loosen Up

Perhaps you will want to have a family massage exchange in the evening after dinner. Each member of the family can get a massage from the rest of the family on a particular evening of the week. Lay a mat on the floor and light candles around the room to create a relaxing atmosphere. After the person who is to receive the massage is settled on the mat, the other family members gather round and lay their palms gently on the part of the body they will massage. Perhaps one person massages the feet or legs, another the arms or torso, and yet another the face or head. Before everyone begins, recite a verse together, such as "Between-times" (page 104). Then gently begin the massage. It is amazing what a few minutes of nurturing touch can do for both the giver and receiver. Take a look at the massage books listed in the "Great Books for Parents" section of the Appendices (page 207).

Cloudy Imaginings

Be observers of the sky! This is a natural pastime for children who pause to read a story from the cloud formations. The shapes and colors transform from minute to minute, and when you and your child become expert cloud watchers, you will discover subtleties of color you never knew the sky held. Find a poem about clouds or the sky and read or recite it together. Then lay together on the ground or sit looking out the window in silence. At the end of your silence, tell each other what you have seen.

Passageways for Parents: Quiet

Have you ever noticed how much parents *talk*? How many questions we ask our children everyday? Children live most fully in the physical and feeling realms. When we pepper them with questions, we are drawing them into the adult world of the intellect, which thrives on information gathering. Quiet pauses in our communication facilitate our willingness to simply be with one another and experience the world more fully in the present moment. Although there are times when questions are necessary and appropriate, I have been surprised to see how often I am able to transform my questions into clear, brief statements (or nonverbal gestures). Also, when my children come to me with unending questions about the world, instead of feeling obligated to give them "the answers," I prefer to guide them to consider the possibilities from their own world view. A friend told me of a kindergarten teacher who responds to children's questions with the pondering phrase, "I wonder, I wonder . . . " In her silence she is delighted at the discoveries the children make, discoveries built on their own inner wisdom.

Another important consideration for ensuring quiet and peace for each family member is to provide a space where each of you may retreat for some alone time. Perhaps you can work as a family to help each member create such a haven for themselves. A bedroom can serve well for moments of centering if the atmosphere is calm and uncluttered. If children share a room, clear other spaces in your home for this purpose. When children help to create a quiet haven for mom or dad as well, they are much more likely to respect your need for privacy and quiet when you retreat to that space.

Verses for Quiet

▶ **Nest of Silence**

Quiet now, we pause to rest,
Silence is our tranquil nest.
Our movement stilled, our voices cease,
We bathe our souls in quiet peace.

▶ **Betweentimes**

Betweentimes:
> *a breathing space,*
> *a quiet spell,*
> *a peaceful face.*

Betweentimes:
> *the unheard sound,*
> *the unvoiced song,*
> *the level ground.*

Betweentimes
> *is where I go*
> *to cool my heels,*
> *idle and slow . . .*

> *Time   between   time.*

▶ **Mother Earth Calls Us**

The grass is a whisp'ring bed of green,
> *Mother Earth calls us to rest.*
The breeze carries time to a place unseen,
> *Mother Earth calls us to rest.*
The trees are rustling a lullaby,
> *Mother Earth calls us to rest.*
Our waking dreams move 'cross the sky,
> *Mother Earth calls us to rest.*

▶ *The Cave of Mum* (A Drumming Chant)

(Start by beating a drum, or your thighs, in rhythm. Then join with the verse. Repeat the verse, getting softer as you go. To end, continue beating the drum in rhythm, getting slower and softer, gradually fading.)

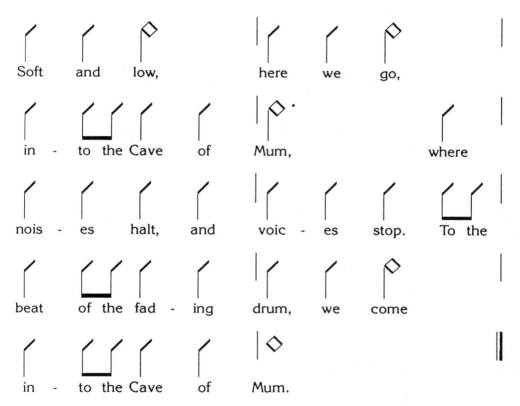

Soft and low, here we go,
in - to the Cave of Mum, where
nois - es halt, and voic - es stop. To the
beat of the fad - ing drum, we come
in - to the Cave of Mum.

▶ *In Stillness*

Take the wind out of your sail,
   take the quickness from your step.
Come sit with me, where stillness
   may lie 'round us like a shawl,
And hold us in the moment
   shining silence covers all.

Songs for Quiet

Golden Silence

Quietly

Shea Darian

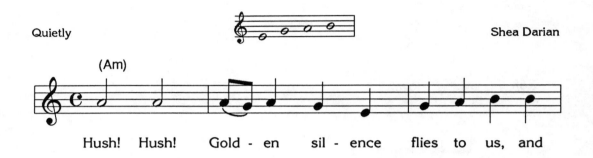

Hush! Hush! Gold - en sil - ence flies to us, and

sil - ence sings: "Lis - ten! Lis - ten!

Feath - ers fall - ing, fall - ing from my gold - en wings."

Silence Comes

Words by
Oliver Wendell Holmes

Shea Darian

(Em)

And sil - ence like a poul- tice comes to

heal the blows of sound. And sil - ence like a

poul - tice comes to heal the blows of sound.

Green Lies the Dancing Water

Smoothly

Source Unknown

Green lies the danc - ing wa - ter,__ Green, pur- ple

barr'd with gold; Brown wing'd my boat flies o'er her, __

Brown wing'd, while out the wa - ter; White the keel, the__

curl- ing wave- let__ toss- es high spray - ing round._____

Quiet Moments

Gently

Shea Darian

*1. Qui- et as the wings of a but- ter - fly,_____
2. Qui- et as the clouds that are drift- ing by,_____

qui - et as the gent - ly fall - ing snow._____
qui - et as the rocks____ by the sea._____

Qui - et as the light of a fire - fly,_____
Qui - et as a mist 'cross a coun-try road,_____

qui - et as a seed starts to grow._____
qui - et as the wind in the trees._____

*You and your child may wish to create your own verses, utilizing images you discover in your quiet interludes.

Quiet! Quiet!

Text revised

German Folksong

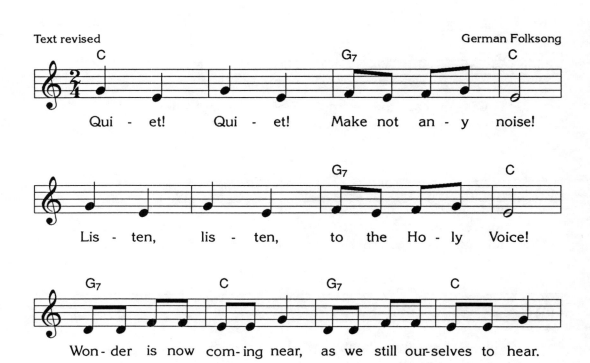

Qui - et! Qui - et! Make not an - y noise!

Lis - ten, lis - ten, to the Ho - ly Voice!

Won - der is now com - ing near, as we still our-selves to hear.

Qui - et! Qui - et! Make not an - y noise!

Stories for Quiet

The Snail's Spell *by Joanne Ryder* (2 - 8)

By the simple text, we are asked to join a child on a silent journey to become a snail in the garden. (New York: Puffin Books, 1988)

The Knee-Baby *by Mary Jarrell* (3 - 8)

The story of a boy who gains a new sibling and thus becomes a "knee-baby," rather than a lap baby. Alan struggles with his feelings of jealousy and isolation as his mother busily attends to his sister. There are a wealth of tender moments that culminate in Alan climbing up into his mother's lap to share some quiet moments and have her "all to himself." (Take note in the scene when Alan almost begins to cry, that the line "These are bad signs," may be changed to "These are crying signs.") (Toronto: Farrar Straus & Giroux, 1973)

Daydreamers *by Eloise Greenfield* (4 - 10)

Sensitive illustrations and poetry reveal the gift inherent in the art of daydreaming. (New York: Dial Books for Young Readers, 1981)

The Other Way to Listen *by Byrd Baylor* (4 - 12)

A child discovers a capacity to listen to nature in a new way, through the guidance of an experienced listener. (New York: Macmillan Children's Book Group, 1978)

Your Own Best Secret Place *by Byrd Baylor* (4 - 12)

Byrd discovers someone's secret place in the hollow of a cottonwood tree and develops a friendship with the absent William Cottonwood. Byrd tells of the secret places of others she has known. (New York: Macmillan Children's Book Group, 1979)

Matthew's Meadow *by Corinne Demas Bliss* (8 - 12)

Matthew's grandmother cleared a meadow in the forest long ago, so a person could sit and see the open sky. Matthew is nine when, for the first time, a red-tailed hawk speaks with him and begins to help him unravel some of life's greatest mysteries. Each year at blackberry time, Matthew meets the hawk in the meadow and is given a message that helps him to awaken all of his senses and to hear, touch, and experience life beyond the boundaries we too willingly accept. (Orlando: Harcourt, Brace & Co., 1992)

A Quiet Time Tale to Spin

"The Boy Who Learned to Listen"

Once upon a time, in Switzerland, there was an old count who lived with his son. Try as he might, the man could not teach the boy a thing of importance. The boy seemed too stupid and slow to ever amount to anything. Finally, when the old man could stand it no longer, he said to his son, "I have tried to get through to that dull head of yours, but it is no use. You must go away and study with a great teacher. It is time for you to wake up and learn something about the world!"

The boy went far away to study in another city with this great teacher. A year later, when he came home, his father was beside himself with curiosity.

"Well, my child," he said, "tell me what you have learned."

"Why, Father," replied the boy, "I have learned to listen to the dogs. When dogs bark, I know what they are saying."

The father threw up his hands. He could not believe his ears! "If that is all this teacher has taught you, I shall send you away to another teacher in another city, who will teach you things of importance about the world — not what the dogs say when they bark!"

The boy went off to study with a second teacher. Again he stayed a year, and again when he returned home, his father asked what he had learned.

The boy told him, "Why, Father, I have learned to listen to the birds. Now I know what the birds are saying when they sing."

Again the father could not believe his ears. "The birds!" he cried. "You know what the birds are saying! I have never heard of such a thing! You should be ashamed, wasting time and money to learn nothing! I shall give you one last chance. I will send you to a third teacher, but if you refuse to learn this time, I will send you away, and you will not be welcomed in this home again."

A third time the son went off to a new city to study with a new teacher. When he returned home, and his father asked what he had learned, the boy replied, "Why, Father, I have learned to listen to the frogs. When the frogs croak, I know what they are saying."

The father jumped up and down in rage, called for his servants, and told them, "This boy is too stupid to be my son. Take him into the forest and do away with him!"

The servants took the boy into the forest. They loved the boy deeply and could not do as the father asked. Instead they gave him a satchel of clothes and food, and told him to travel far away where he would be safe from his father's anger. The boy thanked the servants, and for a time he wandered about the countryside.

One day at twilight, he came to a pond where he heard some frogs croaking. He listened carefully and heard the frogs say, "Your sorrow may end today. Walk down this path, to the three giant oak trees. Climb up over the hill there, and down below you shall find a magnificent castle. When you reach it, be sure to request lodging for the night."

The boy was puzzled by the frogs' message, but he did as they told him. He walked down the forest path, past the three giant oaks, up the hill, and sure enough, when he looked down from the hilltop, there was a splendid castle, where the boy requested lodging for the night. The king of the castle agreed to assist him, but only on one condition. The king said, "You may lodge here, if you are willing to stay in the old dungeon. But I must be honest with you — there are wild dogs that prowl there. We hear them howling all the time, and each day we must offer them a person to devour so they will leave the rest of us in peace. We live in constant fear and sorrow, for the dogs have cost us many lives."

The boy did not hesitate. He asked for some food to feed the dogs and insisted that the barking dogs would not hurt him.

When the boy was lowered into the dungeon, the dogs gathered around him with their tails wagging. The boy spoke to them kindly, and they ate the food he offered. In the morning everyone was surprised to see that the dogs had not harmed him. "You see," he explained to the people, "I have listened to the dogs in their own language. They have told me that they are cursed by a magic spell, which forces them to stand watch over a treasure buried in the dungeon. When the treasure is dug up, the dogs will be set free from this evil curse. From the dogs I have learned where the treasure is and how I may dig it up."

The people rejoiced and the king promised great rewards.

The boy recovered the treasure easily, for he had listened well to all the dogs had told him. Now there was a chest full of gold to enjoy, and the wild dogs went away to live peaceably. The king put on a great feast, and there he asked the boy to live at the castle as his son to help him guide the people of the land. The boy hesitated. He did not know if he was worthy to sit beside the king, and even so, he did not know if he wanted to. Just then, two snow-white doves flew down and landed on the boy's shoulders. They sang sweetly in his ears, "You have learned to listen well. This is the gift of a wise ruler. And we will always be here to assist you."

And so, the boy agreed to live as the king's son, with his feathered friends to call upon whenever he needed them. The boy grew to love the king, and the two ruled together in peace and harmony.

(An adaptation of a tale from the Brothers Grimm, told by Shea Darian)

6 ◗ Skinned Knees, Broken Hearts

Celebrating Healing

'Healing is a matter of time,
but it is sometimes also a matter of opportunity.'

— Hippocrates

Celebrating Healing

The Band-Aid fetish. My daughter Morgan was no exception. By the time she was two, whenever she got a bump or scrape, she made a beeline to the cabinet where the Band-Aids were kept. An expected childhood passage, like the tooth fairy or dandelion-puff wishes. The Band-Aid: simple strip of gauze and plastic, magical healing device of childhood.

To seek out a gesture of comfort so readily — I admire that in children. Who among us does not need the timeless embrace, the compassionate kiss, the gentle healing of the sympathetic eye? Perhaps those of us grown old and tall have forgotten. Forgotten how to meet our pain. Our children remind us.

A friend who is a massage therapist told me of a technique called Ortho Bionomy. In this technique, muscular stiffness and pain are treated by moving the surrounding tissue *toward* the location of the discomfort. The increased tightness sends a clear message to the brain that the area is under stress. The brain sends a message back to the muscles to release themselves. Thus, the increased tightness leads to healing.

After hearing this, I wondered what would happen if I applied this principle in my parenting. What if I began assisting my children (and myself) to move *toward* our injuries rather than away from them? I suspected that if we moved toward our hurt, sadness, anger, frustration, a clear message would be sent to our hearts that the emotion was in need of release. I imagined that moving into our pain could lead to healing.

It is a sunny autumn morning. I fill a bowl with water, set it on a table in our living room. Morgan and I gather pine cones and a bouquet of flowers to place near the bowl. The morning cycles onward, and Morgan comes running, sobbing with a scrape on her arm. I guide her to our "blessing bowl," dip my fingers in the water, sprinkle a few drops near her injury. Gently, I hold my hand over the wound and impart a song of blessing:

> "Healing, healing, healing water,
> Healing, healing, healing tears,
> Bidding good-bye to the hurt in your eyes,
> Farewell to the pain, hello gentle rain." [*]

During our blessing, I witness the tension leaving Morgan's body. Her face becomes peaceful. We linger for a moment in the turning, a conversion that soothes the spirit as well as the body. Morgan slides from my arms, eager to move on with life. Her heart has been revived in that place where healing finds a home.

---

[*] *The music for this song appears on page 127.*

Simple Rituals to Celebrate Healing

A Bowlful of Healing

Choose a special bowl as your family "blessing bowl." Fill it with water. Use it to assist you in responding to your child's minor daily injuries. Add rosewater, a few drops of essential oil of lavender, or flower petals. (Change the water and rinse the bowl often to keep your blessing water fresh.) Choose verses and songs to impart when you use the healing water. Relaxing melodies and gentle rhythms restore a sense of well-being. Hold your hand over your child's bump or scrape tenderly and guide your child to visualize the hurt being released and healing being absorbed by their body. If your child is experiencing an emotional wound, hold your hand over their heart.

Get Out the Hankies

When your child cries, affirm their crying as a natural, positive expression. Talk to your child about how tears help the hurt to flow away. If your child is older, explain how tears restore the chemical balance in our bodies and release stress. Make simple handkerchiefs out of flannel or some other soft material. Give them to your child for crying times and runny noses.

A Healing Basket

Fill a basket with Band-Aids, aloe gel, handkerchiefs, tweezers, clippers, massage oil, arnica salve, or whatever other healing devices you use in assisting your child to heal their daily wounds. Put the healing basket up on a special shelf and take it down whenever a family member needs to soothe a bump or scrape. You may also want to wrap some healing herbs in a piece of cloth and tie it with a ribbon. Your child can sniff this while you are tending a physical wound. Especially soothing herbs are lavender, chamomile, and hops.

Name the Pain

Since children love to acknowledge even the slightest scrape, one fun-filled way to validate these minor wounds is to name them. A scraped cheek might become a "strawberry cheek," a wart might become a "frog's kiss," and a splinter might become a "wee elf's needle" that was misplaced. In this way you can bring humor and fantasy to the situation, and your child can claim the pain as part of the day's experience.

The Balm of Calm

Remain calm as you respond to your child's distress. Do not move into the pain with them. Confidently guide your child into a soothing pause. Rock your child in a porch swing or rocking chair or lie together for a few moments to re-center both of you. An atmosphere of peacefulness enables the healing of body and spirit.

Watery Womb

After an especially trying day with your child, run a warm bath for your child. Use natural bubble bath or a few drops of essential oil of lavender. Rub your child's back with a natural sponge or back scratcher. The calming properties of water are extraordinary.

Is There a Doctor in the House?

If your child is ill or injured, you may want to create an improvisational exchange called, "Is There a Doctor in the House?" Use a puppet or dress up as a doctor and do "daily rounds" when you check and chart the "patient's progress." Suggest methods of treatment: reading a new book, playing a board game, writing a letter to a friend or relative . . .

Healing Light

Choose a special candle for your child, perhaps as a birthday gift. Light the candle with your child when they are sick or struggling in some way. With a younger child, you may wish to share a verse or song of healing. With an older child you may wish to talk about the physical or emotional pain, and pray a healing prayer.

Passageways for Parents: Healing

Many of us have learned to ignore our unpleasant emotions for so long, we have developed the habit of overlooking or suppressing these emotions in ourselves — and in our children. When your child is hurt, take note how you respond to your child. Do you allow your child to cry and express frustration with you, or are you uncomfortable with these kinds of emotional displays? Do you try to diffuse your child's hurt with jokes and play? Do you catch yourself saying things like, "You'll be all right," "It's no big deal," or "What a tough head you have . . . you didn't even cry"? Or do you describe what happened, with direct statements like: "That loud noise scared you," "Sometimes it's hard to say good-bye," or "A skinned knee can really sting"? Using direct statements can help to validate the reality of a child's pain.

However much we would like to ignore it at times, the fact is: We cannot make our children's pains go away. Identify the ways you diffuse, ignore, or suppress the hurts your child experiences and find ways to teach your child that unpleasant emotions are a natural response to the frustrations and disappointments of daily living.

It is also helpful for our children to witness our willingness to nurture ourselves and to seek out the help we need when we are hurt physically or emotionally. When you are ill or hurt, ask yourself how your child could assist you. Could your child bring you a glass of juice? Read you a story? Rub your feet? Prepare a simple meal? If, in our families, we are able to value the spectrum of human emotion and experience, we create room for self-acceptance. When we affirm our pain, there is no need to get stuck in it. Life is a continuous cycle of death and rebirth, tearing down and building up. Our bodies and emotional cycles reflect this as well.

Verses for Healing

▶ *Downpour*

When I am sad,
I want to cry
> *a puddle*
> *a river*
> *an ocean*
> *of tears.*

A downpour:
> *my sadness*
> *my anger*
> *my fears . . .*

Then the storm rolls over,
and a rainbow appears.

▶ *When I'm Hurt*

Bring me healing ointments,
Bring me herbs to smell,
But mostly bring a gentle kiss
To soothe and make me well.

▶ *House Call*

Is there a doctor in the house,
who can cure this
> *terrible*
> *throbbing*
> *sharp*
> *kind of*
> *awful*
> *prickly*
> *feeling*

I have on my behind?
Never mind . . .
I sat on my brother's porcupine.

❯ *Nursing Your Wounds*

I will breathe new life upon you
        when your heart is sinking low,
I will wipe your brow and kiss your eyes
        'til the sadness decides to go,
And I'll stand strong beside you
        as you learn from sorrow's pain,
That like the birds in springtime —
        your joy will come again.

Healing Water

Text revised   Traditional German

Heal - ing, heal - ing   wa - ter   for my   lit - tle

daugh - ter,   Heal - ing, heal - ing   has be - gun,
(son, _____)

Now   the   pain   be   gone,   be   gone.

Blow the Aching Out

Moderately

Shea Darian

When you get a burn, sting, bump, bite, pinch, or scrape, Take a deep breath and blow the ache a - way. Breathe in, [*take in breath*] blow out, [*blow out*] do it a - gain. Blow the ach - ing out and take the heal - ing in.

Water of Life

Peacefully

Shea Darian

Wat - er of Life, —————— flow from my eyes, ————— Sing me sor - row's song, Show me the way of tears that re - veals my deep - est long - ing.

Loving Arms

Gently   Shea Darian

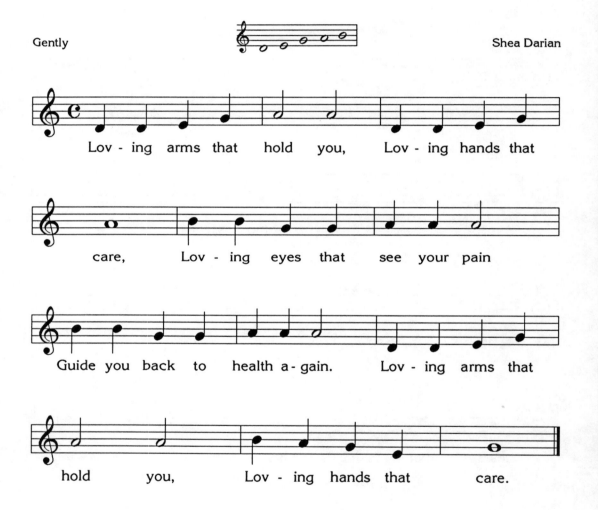

Lov - ing arms that hold you, Lov - ing hands that

care, Lov - ing eyes that see your pain

Guide you back to health a - gain. Lov - ing arms that

hold you, Lov - ing hands that care.

A Healing Blessing

Soothingly

Shea Darian

Heal- ing, heal- ing, heal- ing wa - ter,

Heal - ing heal - ing, heal - ing tears,

Bid- ding good - bye to the hurt in your eyes, Fare-

well to the pain, Hel - lo, gen-tle rain.

Stories for Healing

The Tiny Patient by Judy Pedersen   (3 - 8)

> A simple story about a girl and her grandmother who find a wounded sparrow.
> The two take the bird in, make a nest for it, feed it, and wait for its wing to
> heal. Finally, the bird is well enough to fly away. (New York: Alfred A. Knopf,
> 1989)

Wilfrid Gordon McDonald Partridge by Mem Fox   (3 - 8)

> A boy who lives near an old folks' home has a friend there who has "lost" her
> memory. Wilfrid decides to collect some memories for her, since she has lost
> her own. His gifts jar the woman's memories of days gone by, which she
> shares with Wilfrid. (Brooklyn, NY: Kane/Miller Book Publishers, 1985)

Grandfather's Face by Eloise Greenfield   (3 - 9)

> Tamika's grandfather is an actor, and though his gift has brought her much
> joy, she is faced with her fears that her grandpa might change into a person
> who will not love her. On one of their "talk-walks," her grandfather helps her
> toward understanding. (New York: Philomel Books, 1988)

The Tenth Good Thing About Barney by Judith Viorst   (4 - 9)

> A young boy's cat dies, and his mother asks him to think of ten good things
> about Barney to tell at the funeral. The boy can only think of nine, until he
> and his father talk about what happens to living things that are returned to
> the ground. (New York: Alladin Books, 1971)

Thundercake by Patricia Polacco   (4 - 9)

> When a young girl is frightened of a thunderstorm, her grandma pulls her out
> from under the bed and teaches her how to count between lightning and
> thunder so they will know how long they have until the storm hits. Meanwhile,
> they gather and mix all the ingredients for a "thundercake," which must be
> in the oven before the storm comes. In this way the girl's fear is overcome.
> (New York: Putnam Publishing Group, 1990)

The Acorn People *by Ron Jones* (9 - 12)

A true story of a counselor's experiences with special-needs children at summer camp. The book reflects the pride, struggle, accomplishment and passion the children experience in their endeavors to climb a mountain, put on a watershow, and meet the frustrations and pleasures of camp life. (New York: Bantam Books, 1976)

The Secret Garden *by Frances Hodgson Burnett* (9 - 12)

A cholera epidemic leaves Mary Lennox, a strong-willed and spoiled child, orphaned in India. She is sent to her uncle's manor in Yorkshire and is given little attention. When she meets her cousin, Colin, her view of herself and life changes. Mary also discovers a friend named Dickon, who helps her nurture the manor's hidden and unkempt garden. Mary, Dickon, and the manor's old gardener transform the garden with life and passion. Although there are many editions of this magical tale, I have listed one I like especially well for its illustrations. (Boston: David R. Godine, Publisher, 1987)

A Healing Tale to Spin

"The Seven Ravens"

A woman and man had seven sons, but no daughter. They wished deeply for a girl child, so when the woman became pregnant again and a baby girl was born, the two were very happy. And their seven sons were glad to have a sister at last. However, the girl was born small and sickly, and because her parents did not know if she would live, they wished to baptize her right away. The father sent one of the sons with a pitcher to fetch water from the well. In excitement, the other six brothers went with him. They all wanted to be the one to fetch the water for their sister's baptism, but as they pushed one another in order to be first, the pitcher fell into the well. They stood and gazed down into the well, too dumbfounded to move and too frightened to return home, for fear of what their father would say.

At home, their father grew anxious, and wondered: "What could those boys be doing? They must be playing and have forgotten why I sent them." Because he was upset over the state of his little daughter, he shouted out, "I wish all seven of them would turn into ravens!" As soon as he spoke these words, he heard the sound of flapping wings and went outside to see seven coal-black ravens flying away.

The mother and father were deeply sad over the loss of their sons. But as much as the father wished it, he could not undo the curse. Their little daughter helped to heal their sadness, for she soon grew healthy and strong. She was a delight to her parents and brought much joy to the household.

Her parents never spoke to her about her seven brothers. She thought of herself as an only child, until one day she heard some people in the town talking about her and how she was to blame for the curse that had fallen on her brothers. She ran home to ask her mother and father if this were true.

Her parents knew it was time to tell the child what had happened the day of her birth. When she heard the story, she was beside herself with grief, and although her parents pleaded with her not to blame herself, she could think of nothing else from sun-up to sun-down. She knew she must try to find her brothers and save them from their misfortune.

The girl packed a satchel with a ring given to her by her parents, a jug of water, a loaf of bread, and a little chair to sit upon when she needed to rest. She journeyed from this place to that, searching far and wide for her poor brothers. Finally, she reached the end of the world. So she journeyed on to the sun, but it was burning hot and no place for a child. She journeyed then to the moon, but the moon was a cold and lonely place.

She hurried on to reach the stars and found that the stars were kind and helpful. Each one was sitting on its own little chair, so the little girl pulled out her chair as well and sat down to have a friendly talk with the stars. She told them of her search to find her brothers and was pleased when the morning star pulled out a chicken leg and said: "The glass mountain is where you'll find your brothers. Take this chicken leg and use it as a key to open the gate. Without it, you will never be able to enter."

The girl took the chicken leg, carefully wrapped it in a piece of cloth, and placed it in her satchel. She thanked the stars for their kindness and traveled on to the glass mountain.

When the little girl finally arrived, the gate was locked. She reached into her satchel for the chicken leg, but it was gone. Now she had no key to unlock the gate, so she pulled and pulled at her finger until she pulled it off. She stuck her finger into the keyhole and turned it slowly. The gate opened. So the girl walked into the glass mountain, and there she met a dwarf, who asked, "What are you doing here, my child?"

The little girl replied, "Kind dwarf, I am looking for my seven brothers, the ravens."

"Your brothers are not at home," said the dwarf, "but if you wish to wait, they will return soon."

The dwarf busied himself, preparing dinner for the seven ravens. He set out seven little plates with food and seven little cups with drink. The sister ate a bite from each plate and took a drink from each cup. Then in the last cup, she dropped her ring.

The girl suddenly heard the flapping of wings above her head and ran to hide behind the door. The ravens flew down and hungrily gathered about the table where their food and drink was set. When they saw that someone had eaten from their plates and sipped from their cups, they said, "A human mouth has touched this food." But they were so hungry and thirsty that they ate and drank, until the seventh raven drank to the bottom of his cup and found his sister's ring.

He cried out, "May it be that our sister has come to save us!" Their sister then came out from behind the door, and before her eyes, the seven ravens became human again. At the same moment, the girl's finger was restored. She embraced her brothers, one by one, and joyously returned home with her seven brothers at her side.

(A Grimms' tale, retold by Shea Darian)

7 ◗ Nighttime Pilgrims
Celebrating Bedtime

'Come to the sunset tree!
The day is past and gone.'

— Felicia Dorothea Hemans

Celebrating Bedtime

I remember as a child being frightened of the dark. Seeing a hand beneath the bed, a face upon the curtain — I yelled for Mama, or crawled sideways into the six inches of extra bed beside her while she slept. My father's snoring lured my ears away from the creaks and bumps that easily construed themselves into goblins. Sometimes I still lie awake at night listening to the noises. Imagining what they could be. Old fears die hard.

And yet, I know the night to be a comforter. A cool drink of water after a long, hot journey. The refreshment of pause, the invitation to rest. . . . On a cool autumn evening, as the sun sinks on the edge of the world, I wrap Morgan in a quilt, and we sit on the porch to greet the darkness. Our voices are hushed by the moment in which day and night embrace. Soon we gaze at a sky full of stars and a moon that speaks silently of eternity. I imagine that we are lifted into the magnificent hand of time, swinging like a pendulum. I feel the breath of other times and places, warm upon my cheek. The earth and sky hold us in the web of creation.

Nighttime brings with it a gift to know the world from a different perspective. Perhaps children fear the dark because no one has shown them the path by which to enter into its mystery. Many of us come to darkness as we do silence, with an aversion for the solitude it brings. Darkness slows us down, gives us boundaries for our work and play, touches us with the unknown. Slowness, limits, concession to our blindness — we must welcome all of these if we are to befriend the night and come restfully to the realm of sleep.

Bedtime requires the closing of our eyes and ears and rewards the surrendering of our senses by pouring over us the limitless possibilities of our dreams. Sleep endows us with senses for another way of knowing. In sleep, we may find solutions to problems that startle us in our waking. We may touch and speak with loved ones who have died or who journey far away from us. In sleep, we may commune with the spirit-world. We may uncover emotional and relational issues that need our attention. Our dreaming is a bridge that takes us to the center of spiritual illumination. I want to lead my children peacefully to that bridge. I want to guide them to a world hidden from daylight. Inspire them with the charity of sleep.

Andrew and I creep up the darkened stairs, make our way to our daughters' beds where they lie open-mouthed and sprawling. We kiss their velvet cheeks, pull the covers up to their chins, behold the beauty of sleeping children. A prayer swells in my heart:

"Mother Night, let them run in your fields of darkness,
Let them drink from the cup of your milky moon,
Rock them in your blanket of stars,
And when you depart, kiss their waking souls with your wisdom."

Simple Rituals to Celebrate Bedtime

A Hike in the Night

Take a night walk with your child. Discover the activities and sounds that go on in your surroundings after dark. Perhaps you will want to take a night hike at each full moon, like the mother and her two children in *Walk When the Moon Is Full*, listed in "Stories for Bedtime" (page 147). Find a dark place where the sky is in clear view and do some star-gazing. Wish on a star; sing night songs; tell stories of the stars, the night, and darkness; discover the habits of nocturnal wildlife; learn the constellations and the movement patterns of the nighttime sky and the ancient myths associated with them.

The New Moon Project

Create a ritual to connect you and your child with the waxing and waning of the moon before bedtime. Take notice of the moon's phase and its placement in the sky. Talk with your child about the phases of the moon and the symbolism involved: a new moon represents a time of beginnings, a full moon represents a time of completion. Perhaps, on a new moon night, you and your child can dedicate yourselves to a new project and see it to completion by the night of the full moon.

Quieting Down

Create a nighttime rhythm that helps to move your child into a calm solitude before bedtime. This might involve brushing teeth, lighting a candle in a darkening room, telling a bedtime story, reciting a verse or singing a song, or sharing silent or spoken prayer. Also, a music box might be a quieting transition for a child who does not require your presence after the bedtime ritual is complete.

All in a Day

You may wish to make room in the evening to review the day with your child. Enjoy humorous happenings and fond memories. Be careful not to bring up new topics of conflict at your child's bedtime, although you may want to process through any lingering sadness, anger, or frustration from the day's events. An older child may want to keep a journal in which they write down their thoughts and feelings. Let your child know they can share passages with you if they wish, but that their journal is their own private diary.

Gifts of Darkness

Set aside an evening in which you do not use any electricity or artificial light. Allow yourselves the opportunity to experience the setting of the sun and the darkness that moves in ever-so-gently. Play hide-and-seek, have a conversation in the dark, read a story by candlelight. Talk about the darkness and ask each family member to share how the darkness makes them feel. What are the gifts the darkness brings, as well as the fears?

Rock-a-bye Baby

If you have a young child, acquire a cradle or basket and a doll-sized blanket so your child can perform a ritual with their own "baby" before bedtime. Don't be surprised if the tables turn, and your child begins hushing you so you "don't wake the baby!"

Passageways for Parents: Bedtime

Entering into the realm of sleep is a vulnerable transition for children and requires a caring attitude. Evening is an especially important time to turn off the TV or radio, to slow our movements down, and quiet our voices. If brushing teeth and dressing in pajamas is a prelude for an inspired bedtime ritual, it is usually approached with a feeling of anticipation rather than disappointment. Children thrive on the comfort of a nighttime rhythm on which they can depend.

Young children may require your presence in the room as they drift off to sleep. Sitting and knitting or reading by candlelight in a corner of the room may allow your child to know you are "saving a place for them in the world" while they journey into the dreamy realm. Though a "family bed" is not for everyone, and is a choice that requires clarity and commitment, you may save many a sleepless night by sharing your bed with your child. Having a "family bed" does not mean sleeping with children until they go to college. There are many options to create the profound intimacy that comes with family sleeping. We chose to have a "family bed" with Morgan and Willa until they were eighteen months old. At that age they had each developed a secure sense about nighttime, and the transition to their own bed happened easily. You may wish to consider the gift of a special bedspread, a new doll as a sleeping companion, or the creation of a simple blessing to help your child transition to a new sleeping space.

Evening is also a time to make an assessment of the day: Were there any unkind words spoken that need to be forgiven? Were there special accomplishments or work done by a family member that have gone unrecognized? Is there someone in the family who is struggling in some way and needs attention? It is especially nourishing for children to go to sleep at night with the knowledge that our love for them is constant, that arguments are an inevitable fact of relationships, and that there is acceptance and forgiveness for our conflicts and mistakes.

Verses for Bedtime

▶ *Bedtime Prayer*

There is a candle by my bed,
It dances as with cheer,
While I say prayers for those in need,
And those I hold most dear.

There is a candle by my bed,
It's there to let me know
The Spirit hears my bedtime prayers
In the low light of its glow.

And though I reach to blow it out
When my prayers are done,
That little flame lives in my heart,
'Til the day returns the sun.

▶ *Mother Night*

Mother Night,
Let them run in your fields of darkness,
Let them drink from the cup of your milky moon,
Rock them in your blanket of stars,
And when you depart,
Kiss their waking souls with your wisdom.

▶ To Welcome Night

	Hand Movements for "To Welcome Night"
The dark comes like a blanket,	Extend hands and arms out to sides. With arms straight, bring hands in front of you, chest height.
protecting us at night,	Cross wrists, with palms facing you. Bring palms to rest on chest.
The moon shines *like the heart of God,* *providing gentle light,*	Raise hands and arms above head with fingertips touching, to create round shape of a full moon.
The stars call forth *our sparkling dreams,*	Wiggling fingers, move hands down and out, then with elbows slightly bent, extend arms in front of you, chest height.
like waves upon a shore,	Make the motion of waves with your hands, moving toward right ear.
to greet the nighttime pilgrims *as we journey through sleep's door.*	Place palms together and lay right side of head on them like a pillow.

▶ The Ancient Ones

There is a circle 'round the moon,
Where the ancient mothers sing,
Where the ancient fathers speak
with the tenderness they bring
    to the night.

There is a circle 'round the moon,
    a hazy ring of light,
Where the ancient ones are watching,
    watching,
    watching,
Where the ancient ones are watching
    as the guardians of night.

▶ The Evening Is Coming

The evening is coming.
The sun sinks to rest.
The birds are all flying
straight home to their nests.
"Caw, caw," says the crow
as she flies overhead.
It's time little children
were going to bed.

Here comes the pony.
His work is all done.
Down through the meadow
he takes a good run.
Up go his heels,
and down goes his head.
It's time little children
were going to bed.

— Anonymous

Songs for Bedtime

Candle Glow

Prayerfully

Shea Darian

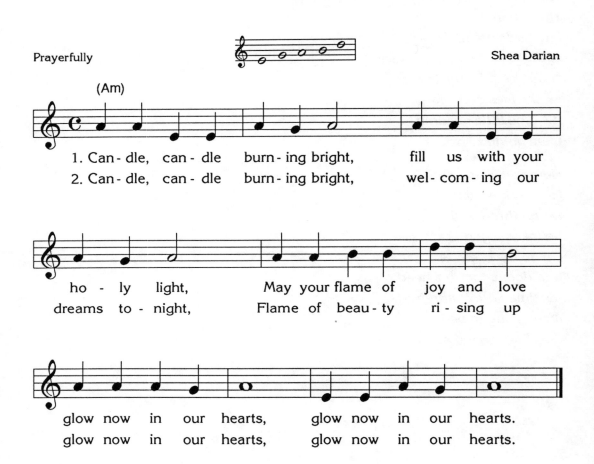

1. Can - dle, can - dle burn - ing bright, fill us with your
2. Can - dle, can - dle burn - ing bright, wel - com - ing our

ho - ly light, May your flame of joy and love
dreams to - night, Flame of beau - ty ri - sing up

glow now in our hearts, glow now in our hearts.
glow now in our hearts, glow now in our hearts.

Round and Round *

3-part round

Source Unknown

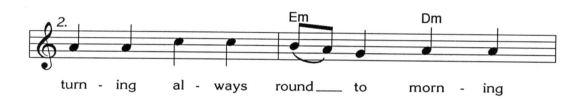

Round and round the Earth____ is turn - ing,

turn - ing al - ways round____ to morn - ing

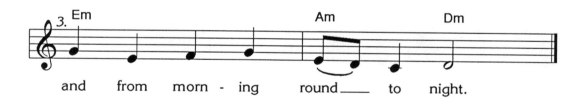

and from morn - ing round____ to night.

*This song is part of the Libana collection *A Circle Is Cast.* Ordering information for Libana songbooks and tapes may be found in the "Great Books for Parents" section of the Appendices under "Songbooks" (page 209).

The Lantern Song

Translated from German
by Margaret Meyerkort

Leslie Poindexter

The sun - light fast is dwind - ling, My

lit - tle lamp needs kind - ling; Its beam shines far in

dark - est night, Dear Lan - tern, guard me with your light.

1.* 2.

Ah--- a--- a--- a,--------- Ah--- a--- a--- a--- a. ------

*Last four measures can be sung as a canon for an echo effect.

Evening Lullaby

Gently

Shea Darian

The an - gel hov- ers ten - der - ly, pulls down the shade, Shad - ows grow long, sleep - y eyes fade in the dusk - light, the moon - light, the star - light, good - night.

Full Moon

Moderately   Shea Darian

Mel - low sage, so fat with love, _____

pol - ished round and spark - ling white,

Joy - ous beams from far a - bove, _____

Touch us with your laugh - ing light.

Stories for Bedtime

Grandfather Twilight by Barbara Berger (2 - 8)

> Each night Grandfather Twilight opens a large chest, removes a pearl from a long strand, and walks to the place where he gives the gift of the moon to "the silence above the sea." Magical illustrations. (New York: Philomel, 1984)

The Midnight Farm by Reeve Lindburgh (2 - 8)

> A counting book in which a mother guides her child around their farm at night to experience images of peace and security. The quality illustrations bring the themes of the story to life. (New York: Dial Books for Young Readers, 1987)

Africa Dream by Eloise Greenfield (3 - 9)

> A child drifts into dreams of long-ago Africa and experiences the marketplace, the music, the dancing of ancestors. And finally drifts off to sleep in the arms of an African grandmother. (New York: Harper Trophy, 1977)

Love You Forever by Robert Munsch (3 - 9)

> The text of this story is heartwarming. It takes us through the years of a boy growing up, and a mother who loves him through all his blunders and phases. Each night, the mother sneaks into the boy's room after he is asleep and sings him a lullaby of unconditional affection. The book ends with an aging mother who needs her son's care and the son's new daughter who receives her grandma's legacy of love. (Buffalo, NY: Firefly Books, 1986)

Dreamcatcher by Audrey Osofsky (3 - 12)

> This story tells of the custom from the Ojibway Indians — to weave dream-catchers for their children. The net catches the bad dreams and lets the good ones through. (New York: Orchard Books, 1992)

Walk When the Moon Is Full by F. Hamerstrom (4 - 12)

> A true story of two farm children who go exploring with their mother on the night of each full moon. Each outing brings cherished discoveries. Read a chapter on each full moon to enhance awareness of the cycle of the year. For another "full moon" collection, see *The Indian Way* listed in "Stories for Mealtime," page 56. (Freedom, CA: Crossing Press, 1975)

Julie of the Wolves by Jean Craighead George (9 - 12)

> Miyax, an Eskimo girl, is lost on the North Slope of Alaska without food or a compass. Through the memory of her father, Kapugen, and a wolf pack who adopts Miyax, she is able not only to survive, but to become self-sufficient and overcome her deepest fears. (New York: Harper Trophy, 1972)

A Bedtime Tale to Spin

"The Star Money"

Once there was a child whose mother and father had died. She had no place to sleep and little food to eat. Her only belongings were the clothes on her back. But the girl was a brave and thoughtful child, and although she had no home or family and no one who cared for her, she did the best she could. One day she set out to find food in the fields, and there she met an old man who said, "Please, I am starving. Give me something to eat." The only food the girl had was a piece of bread someone had given her. She reached into her pocket and gave the man all of it.

The girl traveled on and along the way met a child who was shivering and groaning: "My ears are so cold. Please give me something to keep my head from freezing." The girl took off her hat and gave it to the child.

As she went on her way, she met another child who had no vest, so she gave the child hers.

Farther along, she met a child who had no blouse, and again, she gave her own to the child.

By the time the sun was down, the girl finally reached a forest. There she met another child who asked for her skirt. The kind girl thought for a moment: "Since it is dark, no one can see me. I will give my skirt away as well." She handed her skirt to the other, who thanked her and went away.

The girl stood looking up at the heavens, naked and alone. Suddenly, the stars began to fall from the sky, one after another. And when they landed on the ground, she saw that each star had changed into a shiny coin. Though she had given away all she had on, she saw that she was wearing clothes of the finest linen.

The girl gathered up all the coins that had fallen around her, thanked the heavens, and put the coins in her new pocket, her pocket made of linen.

(A Grimms' tale, retold by Shea Darian)

8 ▶ Endings and Beginnings

Celebrating Weekend Family Time

'All things are connected
like the blood that unites one family.'

— Chief Seattle

Celebrating Weekend Family Time

I remember running home from first grade on Fridays. I hurried because every Friday I knew, when I arrived through our kitchen door, I would meet the aroma of fresh bread coming out of the oven. I waited patiently while my mother sliced it, and then I spread a piece with butter and savored each bite. A highlight of my week: heralding the family time that would come with the week's culmination. The weekend invited our family to gather for Friday night movies and popcorn, Saturday morning chores, trips across town to visit friends. I looked forward to my father's jokes and stories, money-making schemes with my sister, baseball practices with my father and brothers. It was like a deep sigh of completion. A time to remember who we were to one another.

And Sunday . . . Sunday was always a polished, new beginning. Dressed in my patent leather shoes and velveteen dress. Walking to the front of the church sanctuary with the other children where the rotund man with the long robes and laughing eyes would tell us stories about other children, about himself. We would go home after church and sit around a mouth-watering Sunday dinner. (Even after a quasi-vegetarian conversion, I still salivate to think of the roast beef my mother always prepared, smothered with carrots, potatoes, and gravy.)

But the profundity of our Sunday rituals was more than church and roast beef. It was the possibility of an inner turning, a birth of new things to come. The week past, with all its joys and disappointments, was released. The week ahead began with celebration to usher in a fresh cycle of living. There was a lightness about this first day of the week, a day in which music and play flowed naturally.

I can see it in my children as well — the shine that comes to their eyes when we pause in the week to be with one another. Our priority ceases to be defined as forward movement and becomes, instead, a deepening of our affinity and familiarity as family. We experience a cycle of renewal that reaches beyond the cycle of the day, toward the cycles of the moon waxing and waning, toward the balance of time filling and emptying itself. The week asks us to become familiar with endings and beginnings and yet, in the space between these deaths and rebirths, there is an inlet that gives us passage to the present, wherein our children live and breathe.

Simple Rituals to Celebrate Weekend Family Time

Home-grown Gatherings

Create weekend family celebrations, which need not be elaborate. The younger your child, the simpler and more brief these gatherings can be. A gathering might center around a chosen theme or a passage some member of the family is experiencing. One of our most memorable family celebrations was a "weaning ritual" we had for Willa when she was eighteen months old. Andrew read a poem, while I invited Willa to nurse one last time. I offered Willa a tiny round pebble and said, "From the time you were a tiny seed inside me, you were fed from my body." Then I gave her a small ceramic baby her cousin had made and said, "When you were born into this world as a baby, you were fed from my breasts." And finally, I handed her a silver cup, engraved with her name, and said, "Now I give you this cup, so you may feed yourself." We poured rice milk into cups and drank together. Then we sang a blessing for Willa. The whole celebration lasted about seven minutes, yet it is a profound memory in the life of our family.

Family Treasures

Plan a weekly interlude to consider your family identity. Choose or write a family song or verse to begin this time together. You may wish to make a family scrapbook that might include a family tree or stories about your family past, present, and future, or you might draw or paint a family "crest." Consider creating an ongoing project together, such as a family quilt made one square at a time that reflects family interests.

Festive Feast

Choose one meal each week as a feast of celebration. The Jewish sabbath dinner is a profound example of such a tradition. If you practice a religion or have a spiritual focus in your family that holds a day of the week sacred, you may want to cook a special meal on that day or the preceding evening. The significance of the gathering will be heightened if each family member contributes to the festivities. You may want to include specially selected readings and songs as part of the celebration.

Remember When

You may want to have an informal family gathering on Saturday evenings to celebrate the close of one week and the beginning of a new one. One-by-one, recall memories from the past week. You may want to re-imagine a scene and describe it or "perform" it in detail for the whole family to enjoy.

Family Hour

Choose a time each week as "family hour," during which your first priority is your whole family sharing quality time together. When you share this time at home, plan ahead so you won't be interrupted. Your time together might include games, storytelling, conversation, working on a project for your home, gardening, or whatever you can imagine.

One-on-One

Meet weekly to create an ongoing journal with your child. Open up a large blank book or spiral notebook so that each of you can write or draw on adjoining pages. Perhaps you will want to sit across from each other, with one of you writing upside-down. You may wish to offer spontaneous contributions, write letters to one another, or choose a theme each week, such as: "Five things I really like about you," "Something I have never told you before," "One of the saddest moments in my life was . . . ." When you have finished, share your journal entries with one another and talk about what you have written or drawn.

Tea Time Celebration

When someone in your family fulfills a special accomplishment, hold a simple celebration. Make healthy snacks, brew some tea, decorate the table with flowers, and dress up for the occasion. Someone may want to recite a poem or perform a song in recognition of the "guest of honor."

Hidden Talents

Plan a family talent show once a month to share poetry reading, storytelling, drama, dance, puppetry or whatever other hidden family talents are waiting to be expressed. You may want to ask friends or neighbors to share in the fun.

Passageways for Parents: Weekend Family Time

One of the biggest culprits in the demise of family time is electronic media. There is no doubt we live in a culture in which most children in this country are internalizing their world view from their daily interactions with the TV, computer, and Nintendo games. This is such a common struggle for parents that it can be disheartening when experts have come out with study after study affirming the ways in which electronic media is hazardous to our children's development.

Children are hungering for a deeper human connection, and if they don't get it from the people in their lives, it is natural that they will turn to mechanized surrogate "parents." If we want our children to grow up with healthy, compassionate capabilities, they need to be surrounded by people who model these capabilities. We need to set aside TV time and create family time in which we may enjoy the simple pleasures of being together without the constant diversion of "electronic entertainment."

Believe it or not, I know a number of families who have decided not to have a TV in the house and are all the better for it. Another option is to keep the TV in a closet or put a cover over it and use it only for occasional programs. We allow our daughters to see a carefully selected program perhaps three or four times a month. The key to cutting down on TV or Nintendo time is simply to have other things to do together.

Think about your family's typical week. Do you create space in your week for special family gatherings? How does your family celebrate the ending of one week and the beginning of another? What other forms of entertainment would your family enjoy together: the art of conversation, storytelling, music-making, games . . . ?

You might also consider the unique needs and rhythms of each relationship within the family circle. Our daughters' rhythms and temperaments are extremely diverse, and although they are great friends, they tend to bump heads if they have not had enough time with "mom" or "dad" by themselves. Take a look at your weekly rhythms and discover the quantity and quality of time you share with your child individually. Children thrive on one-on-one time, in which foundations of intimacy can be nurtured. Setting aside a specific time each week may be one way your child will know they can count on your undivided attention. Whether it is an hour or an afternoon, it will be a cherished weekly interlude.

Verses for Weekend Family Time

▶ The Days Fly Away!

The Sparrow, Sunday, with wings to fly,
  One time the sun moves across the sky;
The Mockingbird, Monday, with wings to fly,
  Two times the sun moves across the sky;
The Turtledove, Tuesday, with wings to fly,
  Three times the sun moves across the sky;
The Whippoorwill, Wednesday, with wings to fly,
  Four times the sun moves across the sky;
The Thrush, Thursday, with wings to fly,
  Five times the sun moves across the sky;
The Falcon, Friday, with wings to fly,
  Six times the sun moves across the sky;
The Sandpiper, Saturday, with wings to fly,
  Seven times the sun moves across the sky.

Seven times the sun, Seven times the day,
  Now the week is done, and the days fly away!
  Fly away! Fly away! The days fly away!

▶ Falling Star, Rising Star

Falling Star   Can be reborn
Saturday night   And now the week
The week fades   Sunday morn
With a flash of light   Rising Star

◗ *Painting Lesson*

She said, "Please, paint a picture
of the way your week has been."
But there's so much livin' in a week,
I scarce knew where to begin.
So instead of paintin' what I did,
*I painted what I **felt.***

Each day had a different feel to it,
      and Sunday was like white velvet.
Monday was a misty lilac moon,
      and Tuesday was hot pepper red,
Wednesday was yellow daffodils,
      and Thursday — an orange bedspread,
Friday was green as onion grass,
      and Saturday — ocean blue.

This is the way my week has been,
the colors of my week have been,
the feelings of my week have been.
How has it been for you?

Songs for Weekend Family Time

Hanging Out the Linen Clothes

Energetically

U.S. Folksong

1. 'Twas on a Mon - day morn - ing, I worked 'long side my dar - ling, A wash - ing out the lin - en clothes, a - wash - ing out the lin - en clothes.

2. 'Twas on a Tuesday morning, I worked 'long side my darling, A-hanging out the linen clothes. . . .
3. Wednesday . . . A-taking in. . . .
4. Thursday . . . A-ironing. . . .
5. Friday . . . A-mending. . . .
6. Saturday . . . A-folding. . . .
7. Sunday . . . A-wearing. . . .

*Could strum an "F" chord throughout.

Prayer of Thanks and Vision

Meditatively

Shea Darian

*1. We gath - er now, lift - ing
2. We gath - er now, lift - ing

up with care, the
up with care, the

thanks we bring to this
hopes we bring to this

cir - cle of prayer.
cir - cle of prayer.

*Sing first verse through. Then one-by-one, offer thanks for the blessings of the past week. Sing the second verse. Then offer your hopes for the week to come.

We Are a Circle

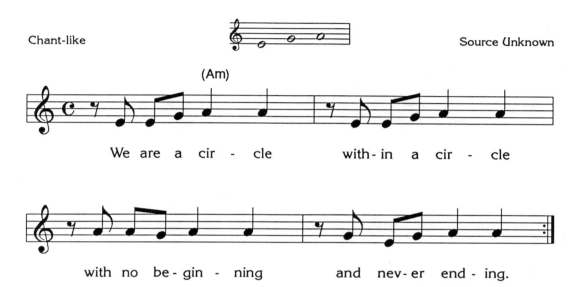

Chant-like

(Am)

We are a cir - cle   with-in a cir - cle

with no be - gin - ning   and nev-er end - ing.

Source Unknown

The Days of the Week

Begin slowly
Faster with each repeat

Shea Darian

We be-gin with Sun-day, the first day of the week,

Sun - day to Mon - day, Mon - day to Tues - day,

Tues- day to Wednes- day, the mid- dle of the week,

Wednes - day to Thurs - day, Thurs - day to Fri - day,

Fri - day to Sat- ur- day, the end of the week.

We Are Dancing Love's Great Circle

Words by Shea Darian*

Tune: "We Are Climbing Jacob's Ladder"

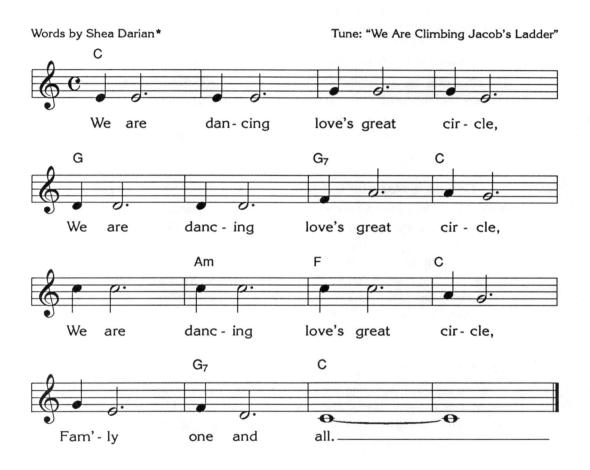

We are dan-cing love's great cir-cle,

We are danc-ing love's great cir-cle,

We are danc-ing love's great cir-cle,

Fam'-ly one and all. _____

2. We will live in peace together. . . .
3. We will speak in truth and listen. . . .
4. We will heal our hurt and sadness. . . .
5. We will live in celebration. . . .

*These lyrics were inspired by the lyrics of "We Are Dancing Sarah's Circle" by Carole Ann Etz, found in *Sing a Woman's Song*, published by the Ecumenical Women's Center, Chicago, IL.

Stories for Weekend Family Time

Owl Moon by Jane Yolen   (3 - 9)

Beautiful illustrations accompany a captivating tale of a child who ventures out with father to experience the late night adventure of owling for the first time. (New York: Philomel, 1987)

The Keeping Quilt by Patricia Polacco   (4 - 10)

The story of a Jewish family, who immigrates to the U.S. from Russia, and the quilt that they make as a remembrance of their Russian roots. The quilt is passed on through four generations and is used as a sabbath tablecloth, a wedding canopy, and a blanket to welcome new babies. (New York: Simon & Schuster, 1988)

Knots on a Counting Rope by Bill Martin, Jr. and John Archambault   (5 -12)

A story in dialogue form between a grandfather and grandson. The two sit by the campfire and tell together the story of the boy's life from birth to the present, including the boy's naming ceremony, and the boy learning to ride and race his horse, even though he is blind. Each time the story is told, they tie a knot in the counting rope. When it is filled with knots, the boy will know the story by heart. You might want to perform this story with an older child as reader's theatre for the whole family to enjoy. (New York: Henry Holt & Co., 1987)

Ashanti to Zulu by Margaret Musgrove   (6 - 12)

An alphabet book depicting the rituals and lifestyles of twenty-six African tribes. The many customs and celebrations recounted here may be an inspiration to identify or create your own family "customs." (New York: Dial Books for Young Readers, 1976)

The Lucky Stone by Lucille Clifton   (8 - 12)

Tee's great-grandmother tells her the fascinating stories of the lucky stone and how the stone was passed along among family and friends. The luck of the stone helped a runaway slave, saved its keeper from death, helped another meet her husband, and finally the hundred-year-old magic is passed on to Tee. (New York: Dell, 1979)

A Family Time Tale to Spin

"The Water Nixie"

One Sunday afternoon a family was enjoying a picnic in the country. As the sun began to set, Mother and Father gathered their belongings to return home. They called out to Little Brother and Little Sister, who were playing by a well. But just then, the children's ball fell into the water. When the children chased after it, they fell into the well.

At the bottom they met a water nixie who grabbed them and said, "Now you shall come to my house and work for me from sun up to sun down!" And off she took them, through a long, dark tunnel, to a part of the country they did not know. Little Brother and Little Sister were frightened and sad, for they missed their parents greatly.

On Monday morning the nixie woke them before the sun came up and put them to work. Little Sister was told she must spin some filthy, tangled flax and carry water in a bucket that had no bottom. Little Brother was told to chop down a tree with the dullest axe he had ever seen. The nixie fed the children her leftover scraps and ordered them to sleep on the floor of the chicken coop. They did all this for five days without a word of complaint, but finally on Friday evening, when work was done, they lay on the floor of the chicken coop and made plans to escape.

The nixie had given them orders for Saturday chores, since she would be off to market early in the morning. After she left, Little Brother and Little Sister ran away to find the passage that would lead them back to the well.

When the nixie returned from market, she realized what had happened and began to run after the children. When Little Brother and Little Sister saw her coming, the girl reached into her pocket and threw her brush in front of the nixie. The brush turned into a large mountain covered with bristles, which the nixie found difficult to climb. Just as the nixie made it over this mountain, Little Brother reached into his pocket and threw a comb in front of her. The comb turned into a large mountain covered with jagged teeth that poked at the nixie, but she managed to climb over it.

Finally, Little Sister reached into her pocket again and threw a mirror in front of the nixie. The mirror became a shining mountain of glass, which was so slippery the nixie knew she would never be able to cross it. She thought it best to run home and get her axe to shatter the mountain to pieces. By the time she returned, the children were out of sight. Little Brother and Little Sister found the passage to the well, and once they were at the bottom again, they yelled for help. Their parents, who had been searching for them all week long, heard their cries, threw a rope to them, and pulled them back up the well. The family returned home and prepared a hearty breakfast feast, overjoyed to be together once again.

(An adaptation of a tale from the Brothers Grimm, told by Shea Darian)

FOR PARENTS ONLY

9 ▶ Walking on Sacred Ground

Celebrating Personal Renewal

'Fortunately [psycho]analysis is not the only way to resolve inner conflicts. Life itself still remains a very effective therapist.'

— Karen Horney

Celebrating Personal Renewal

My friend is a mother of two children. Her partner works outside the home, and she spends long hours caring for her little ones. She does not believe in microwave dinners or disposable diapers. She does believe in wholesome meals that require time to prepare and hanging her clothes on a line to dry.

My friend tells me she does not even have time to brush her hair. I say that is why she must. I tell her to find time to brush her hair twice. She laughs and dismisses my suggestion with a puzzled groan.

I can envision my friend clearly: dinner dishes dripping dry, baby asleep, the two-year-old playing with daddy before bedtime. I see my friend sitting in front of a mirror, brush in hand, stroking through her sandy brown hair. She looks at her face in the mirror, sees herself for the first time that day. Nurturing herself through this simple act, my friend weeps at the sight of her spirit, surfacing out of the busyness and unexpressed emotion.

Just as it is with my friend, the hugeness of my task as homemaker sometimes overshadows my reverence for the task — this labor of love. Too often I witness fragments of myself (parent, partner, child, friend) flying out to meet people. I feel unable to bring my whole self to these encounters for fear of expending all my energy in one place.

When this fragmentation occurs, I begin to hear voices inside my head: voices of expectation, criticism, longing . . . and, finally, a voice that tells me I must create "sacred ground" upon which to walk, a place to gather the fragments of myself and be fed by the Spirit of Life. My soul requires time for reflection, quiet passage, self-communion.

Spiritual centeredness requires us to know and nurture ourselves. Creating time to "brush our hair" can transform us. In those precious moments when we see what is true, or what could be true in our lives, we may find ourselves living our whole day differently.

Simple Rituals to Celebrate Personal Renewal

Mirror, Mirror

In the quiet of the evening, when the children are snug in bed, sit in front of a mirror and brush your hair gently. Meditate upon the events of the day. Were there any important lessons or especially inspiring moments? How did you feel today? How did you express these feelings? What personal needs were or were not met today? How could your unmet needs be met tomorrow or in the coming week?

Light for the Path

Light a candle and offer prayers, asking the Spirit of Illumination

. . . for guidance in your parenting

. . . for the well-being of a friend who is celebrating a birthday or anniversary

. . . for the safety of a friend who is traveling

. . . for comfort as you remember a loved one who has passed on

. . . for support of a person in need

. . . for joy as you celebrate a special accomplishment or passage

. . . for grace so that your acts of love will be like a glowing fire warming your home

. . . for whatever your heart can imagine

Handful of Healing

When we are busy caring for home and family, it is too easy to overlook the aches and pains that tell us to slow down and take care of ourselves. When you feel discomfort or pain in your body, pause from your daily tasks. Lie down and rest for a few minutes. Oftentimes the pain will subside in response to this kind of self-nurturing. You may wish to speak a healing verse, enlist the help of a family member for a few minutes of massage, or if possible, soak in a warm bath by candlelight to heal your body and mind.

Living Water

Reflect upon water as a symbol of the Spirit of Life, for water is the source and sustenance of all life. Fill a pitcher with water. Reflect on the nourishment and cleansing water brings us. Keep your pitcher on hand throughout the day for times when you need encouragement. Pour a cup of water and speak an affirmation, such as, "I am nourished and refreshed by the Spirit of Life." Or you may want to keep a bowl full of fresh water to use as a "prayer bowl." We keep a bowl near the back door on a small wooden shelf. When I feel the need for clarity and centeredness, as I enter or exit the house, I dip my fingers in the water and say this blessing: "May I enter/exit this house with clear thoughts (*I touch my forehead*), wise words (*I touch my lips*), kind heart (*I touch over my heart*)."

Magic Broomstick

Allow household tools to reflect the state of your soul. A broom, for example, sweeps the floor clean, gets into unseen places to expose dirt, dustballs, and misplaced objects. Next time you sweep, consider one of the following questions: What do I need to sweep from my life? What do I need to expose or rediscover about myself?

Love Letters

Fill a shoebox with letters, quotes, poems, and pictures that reflect the support of the people you love. Bring these out and read them when you need to nurture yourself or muster confidence.

Nurturing the Child Within

When I was browsing around a friend's apartment, I spied a list entitled, "Things to do for the child in me . . . " The list included such pleasures as playing the guitar and singing, trading a massage with a friend, swimming, going for a bike ride, buying a longed-for item of clothing, dancing, calling a special friend . . . Make a list of your favorite activities for fun and relaxation and be willing to indulge yourself once in a while.

Passageways for Parents: Personal Renewal

If we hope to create rhythm and harmony in the lives of our children, we must begin with ourselves. When we are able and willing to nurture ourselves by giving ourselves "alone time" and time with other adults, we cultivate inner resources that allow us to meet our children with a great deal more balance and joy. But reserving "alone time" and deepening intimacy with other adults is one of the most challenging aspects of parenting. Ask yourself: Do I have personal time each day or "retreat time" each week to replenish myself for the task of parenting? Do I share intimate time with my partner? Does my child have other adults in their life to nourish them on a regular basis?

If you have a parenting partner, brainstorm ways you can balance parenting responsibilities with personal needs. Depending on your job situations, you may be able to take turns being the primary parent for your child. Although it may take a great deal of soul-searching, you may wish to consider career or lifestyle changes that will allow you the freedom to give your child the quantity and quality of time you want to give them. If you are the primary caregiver for your child, create a schedule in which you have some time to yourself each day.

Single parents may have more of a challenge finding an intimate friend or relative to share parenting responsibilities. When I was working as a minister before I became a parent, I was impressed by two divorced women I knew in the church community who chose to live and parent their children as a family. If you are parenting and living as the lone adult in a family, make sure there are other adults in your family's life who are worthy of your love and respect, and who can free you for periods of time from the intense energy it takes to parent each and every day.

It is an unfortunate fact that the structure of our society breeds isolation for those of us who choose to stay home with young children. To be a healthy, joyful parent, creating a support network is essential. Seek out others with young children or those who thrive on the company of little ones. Create child care exchanges or bartering situations with people you know and trust.

For nourishment and support, you may wish to find or create significant community outside your immediate family and commit yourself to meeting monthly or even weekly with these folks. Your larger community may be found at a church or synagogue, gatherings of a special interest group, or at a spirituality circle created by people like yourself. "Home-church" (in which families meet in homes and take turns planning celebrations and activities for the children) is an idea that might draw those who wish to have a more intimate experience of what it means to share a "common faith" with others. A Jewish friend of mine is a member of a "havurah," which meets every month in members' homes. They plan half their celebrations to include the children and half for adults only. In this way the whole family can participate, AND the parents have time to reap the intimacy of adult interaction and celebration.

Verses for Personal Renewal

❯ *Prayer of Life*

For at last I believe
life itself is a prayer,
and the prayers we say
shape the lives we live,
just as the lives we live
shape the prayers we say.
            — Ted Loder

❯ *Honoring Our Tears*

Eyes bereft a single tear
are sadder still
than those that weep.

❯ *Prayer for Clarity*

May I enter this house
with clear thoughts,   (touch forehead)
wise words,   (touch lips)
kind heart.   (place open palm over heart)

▶ *Inner Wisdom*

Once upon a time, before the study of theology,
    there was inner wisdom.
Before church buildings
    there was the earth beneath my feet.
Before religious hymns,
    there were the spontaneous chants inspired by the season's blazing colors.
Before preachers,
    there was my grandfather, with his big old picture Bible,
        adding flare and nuance to those old stories
            in a way the preachers could hardly imagine.
But even before the Bible,
    there were stories of my life, and Demetra's and Rebecca's,
        and the little boy who lived down the street.
Before Sunday dresses and Easter hats,
    there were blue jeans and cotton blouses that were made for caressing
        the earth, trees, and railroad tracks that ran behind our house.
Before words and liturgy,
    there was dance and motion . . . circling, jumping, leaping my prayers
        among my friends the trees, the sun, the shadows, the spiders.
Before solemn statues,
    there was the Spirit of Life within, around, and beyond me,
        and there was my mother with her kind words,
            her crystals and her fresh-baked bread from the oven.
Before the baptism of salvation,
    there was the baptism of summer rainshowers,
and before that,
    the baptism of birth in the water of the womb.
Before lines,
    there were circles.
Before ladders,
    there were spirals.
        So I circle and I spiral to the wisdom of my child-self.

Songs for Personal Renewal

I Am Born Anew

Meditatively

Shea Darian

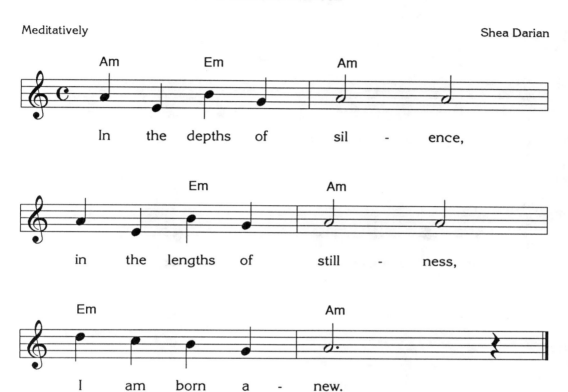

In the depths of sil - ence,

in the lengths of still - ness,

I am born a - new.

Spirit, Move Me

Prayerfully

Shea Darian

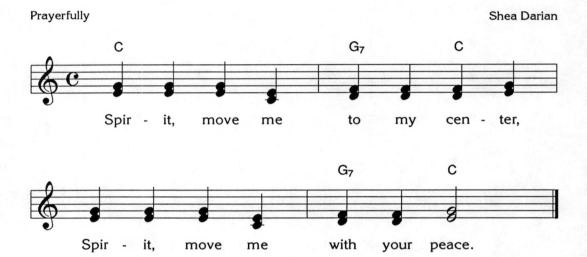

Spir - it, move me to my cen - ter,

Spir - it, move me with your peace.

Now I Walk in Beauty *

Words: Hopi Indian

Now I walk in beau - ty,

Beau - ty is be - fore _____ me,

Beau - ty is be - hind _____ me, A -

bove _____ and be - low me.

*This song is part of the Libana collection *Fire Within*. Ordering information for Libana songbooks and tapes may be found in the "Great Books for Parents" section of the Appendices under "Songbooks" (page 209).

9 ♪ Walking on Sacred Ground   175

Blue Mountain Chant

Words from an Apache chant
Translation by Harry Hoijer

Shea Darian

Big Blue Moun - tain Spir - it,

Big Blue Moun - tain Spir - it,

Home made of blue clouds, ———— I am

grate - ful for that mode of good - ness there.

Truth Encircle Me

Gently

Shea Darian

Truth en - cir - cle me,

Truth be mine, Let

me be truth,

Truth en - cir - cle me,

Truth _____ di - vine.

Stories for Personal Renewal

(Here are some of my favorite storybooks and collections for the child in me. You may wish to find a quiet haven during your alone time and absorb the wisdom and humor in these pages. The first six books listed are appropriate for children, too, depending on their age and interest.)

Hope for the Flowers by Trina Paulus

A caterpillar struggles between following the crowd up the "caterpillar pillar" or risking all he has known to become a butterfly. (New York: Paulist Press, 1972)

I'm in Charge of Celebrations by Byrd Baylor

The author leads us through a year of the personal rituals she has created for herself in the Southwest desert country where she lives. She tells of the events that have led her to celebrate Dust Devil Day, Rainbow Celebration Day, Green Cloud Day, Coyote Day, The Time of Falling Stars, and a New Year Celebration. (New York: Charles Scribner's Sons, 1986)

Lafcadio by Shel Silverstein

A humorous and thoughtful tale about a lion named Lafcadio who discovers that shooting back at the lion hunters beats running for one's life. Lafcadio becomes a skilled shooter, is recruited by a circus owner to perform in his circus, becomes wealthy and famous, and begins to question the path he has chosen. (New York: Harper & Row, 1963)

The Little Prince by Antoine De Saint-Exupery

A fable in which the narrator encounters a little prince from another planet, who in his own search for the secrets of life, teaches the narrator as well. (Orlando: Harcourt, Brace, Jovanovich, 1971)

The Maid of the North by Ethel Johnston Phelps

A collection of feminist folk tales from around the world. (New York: Henry Holt & Co., 1981)

The Man Who Planted Trees by Jean Giono

The story of a successful attempt at reforestation, affirming the strength of the human spirit to heal the earth. (Postmills, VT: Chelsea Green, 1985)

Living by the Word by Alice Walker

> A collection of autobiographical essays that bring depth and insight to the interrelatedness of all of life. Walker meditates on feminist, political, racial, family, lesbian and gay, and ecological issues with sensitivity and conviction. (Orlando: Harcourt, Brace, Jovanovich, 1988)

Mists of Avalon by Marion Zimmer Bradley

> A compelling tale that brings new life to the Arthurian legends. Told from the experience of women such as Guinevere and Morgan of the Faeries. Both eye-opening and magical. (New York: Ballantine Books, 1982)

The Song of the Bird by Anthony de Mello

> A collection of traditional and contemporary parables from a variety of religious traditions that bring insight to our common spiritual journey. (New York: Doubleday, 1984)

A Renewing Tale to Spin

"The Golden Key"

Once upon a time, there was a poor boy who lived with his mother and father. They were growing old, and the boy worked hard to care for them. One cold winter day, the fire in the stove was burning low, and there was no more wood to burn. So, the boy set out with his sled to gather firewood in the forest. The snow was piled high on the ground. The wind bit through his clothes. But the boy trudged along heartily, determined to finish his work.

After his sled was full, the boy noticed his toes growing numb from the cold. He decided to build a fire to warm himself before returning home. As he cleared the snow away, he saw laying on the ground a little golden key. The boy marveled at the key — so small and shiny.

"Where there's a key, there's sure to be a lock," he thought. So he dug and dug down into the earth. Soon, sure enough, the boy came upon a sturdy iron box. He imagined there must be treasures inside, something wonderful and precious! He searched and searched for a keyhole, but try as he might, he could not find one. He threw off his woolen mittens and ran his fingers along the cold, smooth sides of the box. Finally, he found a tiny opening, so small he could barely see it.

"If only the key will fit," the boy whispered, as he slipped the little golden key into the lock. It fit perfectly! He turned the key with a click and slowly, slowly began to open the lid. And now. . . . you'll have to wait until he opens it all the way, so you may see the wonders that lay inside the box.

_____

(A Grimms' tale, retold by Shea Darian)

10 ▶ We Are the Peacemakers

Celebrating Peacemaking

'First keep the peace within yourself
then you can also bring it to others.'

— Thomas à Kempis

Celebrating Peacemaking

A peace activist friend of mine tells me, "If I can create peace with my children, then perhaps I will really learn something." This is a woman who has spent weeks in jail for communicating her convictions of human dignity and freedom, a woman who dreams of working and living in a third world country one day, a woman who has spoken and danced and sung for the cause of world peace. And she is humbled in the presence of her children.

Yes. I know what she means. With our children we are faced with the best and worst in ourselves. Perhaps no one in our lives can inspire our hostility and anger to surface quite as readily and completely as these people we call our daughters and sons.

Since I can remember, I always believed that spanking or hitting a child was wrong. I knew long ago that if I ever became a parent, I would certainly never use such a form of punishment on my children. Then one afternoon, Morgan was tossing and turning at naptime, whining that she didn't need a nap and didn't want to lay down. I slipped into the bed beside her, hoping to calm her. She suddenly turned and punched me with her fist right between the eyes. My emotions blurred. I reacted by slapping her bare shoulder with an open hand. Immediately, we both burst into tears. In four years of parenting, I had never hit either of my children, had always judged parents harshly who did. In that split second, I was faced with that capability in myself. I felt as if something inside me was broken. In a matter of hours, Morgan was playing and singing, as if nothing had occurred. She had seemingly forgiven me and moved on. I, on the other hand, grieved over the episode for days. It took me two weeks to begin to forgive myself.

As I gained perspective on this episode, it became apparent to me that inflicting pain upon children is a way of unleashing inner chaos, using them as a release valve for our own lack of inner peace. What else could possibly lead us to inflict physical, verbal, or attitudinal pain upon our children? Whenever I have responded inappropriately to Morgan or Willa, I can always trace my actions to an unresolved personal issue. My aggression is not about them. They are merely catalysts who help bring it to the surface. On the other hand, when I am at peace with myself, my children can act outrageously, and I am able to respond with a clear mind and heart. I am able to set clear boundaries and offer firm gestures that inspire mutual respect and help to build our relationship as parent and child.

Perhaps you have noticed that there are a great number of children growing up among us with iron-strong wills. These children have to be strong and willful to put forth the kind of energy necessary to set our world aright again. Parenting such children makes us feel at times that we must use an iron hand with them if we are to retain any semblance of order and control. It is easy to feel that if we choose not to wield the iron hand, we will allow chaos to run the household.

These children who are gracing our planet with the gift of the willful act need a generation of parents who are equally as strong and decisive. These children are hungering for guides to help direct the energy forces they bring to the earth — not to smash their energies with an iron hand nor to sit idly by and allow these energies to be unleashed wildly upon the world. But guides who are able to teach peace — respect for oneself, others, our homes, and our world. The elements that produce peace in our selves and our homes are the same elements that produce peace among nations and peoples. Here in our homes, here is the learning ground. And when we create peace with our children, then perhaps we, too, will really learn something.

Simple Rituals to Celebrate Peacemaking

Transforming the Wrong

Everyone needs an opportunity to transform a wrong-doing. Create a ritual for your child to use to turn conflicts into cooperative efforts. When Willa and Morgan hurt one another physically, we sit together quietly for a few moments, and when they are ready, they apologize and face each other, holding right hands and left hands together in a handfasting gesture. Then they speak a simple covenant: "No [hitting] in this house, only talking in this house." The inserted word could just as easily be "biting" or "kicking" or "pinching" or "pushing" or . . . This covenant almost always ends with a giggle or a beaming smile, and they are off running and playing together again.

Attention, Please!

There are more effective ways to get a child's attention than raising one's voice. Children have a capacity for living in the moment, and we will assist our children in making the necessary transitions from one activity to another by being aware of their need to be guided gently. Next time you are struggling to gain your child's focus, try singing their name. Children are immediately drawn to music, especially when they realize it is their name you are singing. How much more refreshing to hear our names sung in a gentle melody, rather than barked out with a harsh voice. A hand on the shoulder or leaning down to whisper in a child's ear are other effective "attention getters." Also, take a look at the song "What'cha Doin'?" in "Songs for Peacemaking" (page 193).

Take Two

Hurting one another occasionally is an inevitable fact of relationships. Use mistakes as an opportunity for learning. Whenever someone in your family has been hurt by another family member, "replay" the action by piecing together the story of each person who was involved. When the story is complete, create a new scene by replaying the action to the point of the conflict and then envision together how the situation might have been resolved differently.

Peace Pilgrims

The peace you create together as a family is a seed for a world in need of peaceful gestures. Discover ways your family can effect a change for a more peaceful world. Gather as a family and reflect upon ways your family values peace, how you live out these values through your daily acts. For example: "We don't hit each other"; "We share our food with one another"; "We clean up after ourselves"; "When one of us is sick, the others care for that person." After you have made a list of these "values in action," consider how you might share these beyond your own home and family. "We don't hit each other" might lead your family to volunteer an hour or two at an agency that works as an advocate for abused children. "We share our food with one another" might lead your family to work at a soup kitchen or breakfast program at a nearby church. "We clean up after ourselves" might lead your family to begin a recycling program for your own home and to share your ideas with friends and neighbors. "When one of us is sick, the others care for that person" might lead your family to minister to those in your community who have the AIDS virus. The possibilities are endless, and the giving gesture is a transformative one. Learning to be a strong individual who can also be a servant to others is a balance worthy of our striving.

Clearing the Air

Use sweet-smelling scents, such as incense or potpourri, to bless your home with peace and tranquillity. It is a Native American custom to burn sage to purify the air. A friend of mine creates herbal "smudge sticks" out of sage, juniper, and cedar, wrapping the herbs with embroidery thread. Use such aromatic tools at the beginning and end of the day, to purify your home after conflict or trouble, or to prepare a room for some special purpose.

Grump-Dump

When you or your child is grumpy, frustrated, or angry, think of ways to release your pent-up feelings without taking them out on each other. Try to push a big tree down. Take a bag of unshelled sunflower seeds and throw them by the handful across your yard or the park lawn (the birds will be happy). Find someone your size to play a game of tug-o-war. Stomp aluminum cans (wearing a heavy pair of shoes). With a willing participant have a water battle (using spray bottles). Run around the outside of your house or apartment building several times. Sing the world's dumbest song at the top of your lungs. Do anything that is *not harmful to someone else*. In this way, you and your child can express yourselves without being destructive.

Passageways for Parents: Peacemaking

We live in an age of "instant answers." We long for the miraculous formula that will cure our ill, the missing piece that will complete our puzzle. With parenting, there is no formula, no puzzle piece that deems the task complete. We are an unfinished breed, like children. We learn mostly through mistakes and fortitude. Falling short of our ideals is inevitable.

One of the greatest challenges in parenting is finding the balance between allowing our children to unfold as unique individuals and setting boundaries for them when they are being destructive to themselves, their environment, or other people. This balance can only be found through experience and by reflecting upon the constant questions that arise as we assist our children in their development: Are my expectations of my child appropriate for their age and stage of development? Am I consistent in my methods of bringing discipline to my child? Do I discipline differently in the privacy of our family than I do when other friends or relatives are around? Do I feel the tools I use are fair and effective for both me and my child?

I have found it helpful, whenever I feel I have responded inappropriately to my children, to talk with Andrew and one or two other friends about the experience. I replay for them what happened. I talk about the issues that led to the episode and consider the unmet needs that may have facilitated it. Were either of us hungry? Tired? Confused? In need of some peace and quiet? Then I talk about how I could have approached the situation differently.

I believe it is important not to keep our parental transgressions to ourselves. Part of our healing and transformation as parents is accepting our human frailties and our ability to make mistakes. Forgiving ourselves and moving on is an important part of growth and change for peaceful parenting. Our children will know if we are striving and growing as parents. The life-affirming gestures we offer them have a way of healing our mistakes.

Of all the reasons I chose Andrew as my marriage partner, none is more significant than his ability to inspire me to laugh at myself — and life. I cherish his ability to see the humor in the comedic tendencies of our family — a family in which each of us is equally as bold and strong-headed as the others. Sometimes when Andrew and I are playing a heated game of emotional tug-o-war, we suddenly turn to look at one another. Someone holds the hint of a smile in their eyes, and we both let out a belly laugh that reminds us not to take ourselves so seriously. I think this is a cornerstone of our marriage and our family.

Family. This is the hardest work we will ever do. Nowhere will we feel such a strenuous pull of responsibility to others, of expectation, of a desire to be understood and accepted. And nowhere is there a greater need to appreciate the divine comedy of the universe that could bring together such an unusual chemistry of character under the same roof.

It is certain there are days laughter will be our saving grace. For our family, laughter is a ritual of release when we find ourselves wading through a strong current of unending blunders and confusion. We throw our heads back and laugh long and deeply with the Spirit of Life. We toss off the heavy weight of all we are not. And light-footed, we move forward.

Verses for Peacemaking

▶ *How Much Is Enough?*

How much is enough of "I Love You,"
How much is enough, would you say?
And how many hundreds of hugs
      would a person require to fill up a day?

How much is enough of "I'll miss you,"
"I need you," and "I wanna kiss you"?
Perhaps just enough is enough . . .
      'cause we need so much of this lovely stuff.

▶ *Welcome Sign*

To all friends who enter here:
May you be humbly blest,
Lay your burdens at the door,
You are an honored guest.

▶ *Prayer for Small Things*

Dear Spirit, hear and bless
The beasts and singing birds
And guard with tenderness
Small things that have no words.
    — Anonymous

▶ *A Peace Blessing*

Blessed are the peacemakers,
for they shall be called
the children of God.
    — Matthew 5:9

❯ Peace Procession

Let us play the pipes of peace
        for all the world to hear,
Let our song ring out with freedom
        to quench all doubt and fear.

Begin the peace procession,
        and people then will come —
when they hear the piping song of peace,
        and the beat of the healing drum.

Let us play upon our pipes
        a peace that's understood
by those of every nation
        who uphold creation's good.

Begin the peace procession,
        march side-by-side and strong,
Our guide will be the Spirit
        of our peaceful, piping song.

Peace Bless this House

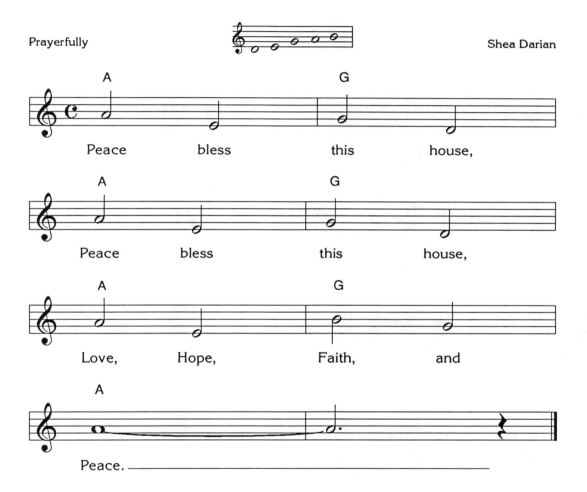

Prayerfully

Shea Darian

Peace   bless   this   house,

Peace   bless   this   house,

Love,   Hope,   Faith,   and

Peace. _____

Family of Mine

A Simple Chant

Shea Darian

Fam - i - ly of mine, teach me to show sad - ness,

Fam - i - ly of mine, teach me to show char - i - ty,

Fam - i - ly of mine, teach me to show an - ger,

Fam - i - ly of mine, teach me to show me.

What'cha Doin'? *

Moderately

Shea Darian

*This song may be used to call a child to you or to get their attention. Of course, you'll have to insert the appropriate name. The child's answer may be sung in a similar melody: "Readin' a book, that's what I'm doin', (3x) what I'm doin', . . ."

Compassionate Heart

2-part round

Shea Darian

Bring forth your gen - tle spark, Il-
lum - ine now the dark. Those
trem - bling in the night, Re -
ceive your shin - ing light.

Shalom Chaverim

3-part round*

Traditional Hebrew Blessing

** Sha - lom, cha - ve - rim; sha -

lom, cha-ve-rim, Sha - lom, sha - lom. Sha-

lom, cha - ve- rim; sha - lom, cha-ve- rim; sha-

lom, sha - lom.

*When sung in unison, sing slowly and gently one time through, then a second time more quickly, with passion.

**Shalom: peace, hello, farewell   Chaverim: dear friends

Stories for Peacemaking

A Place for Ben by *Jeanne Titherington*   (2 - 8)

Beautiful illustrations and a simple text tell the story of Ben whose room has been invaded by his baby brother's crib. Ben decides to create a secret place for himself where he can be alone. He sits in his private space, but soon a feeling of loneliness arises. After he attempts to coax the cat, the dog, mom, and dad to his secret place without any success, he is visited by his baby brother. (New York: Greenwillow Books, 1987)

Sisters by *David McPhail*   (2 - 8)

The story of two sisters who were different AND very much alike. The everyday rituals of the two sisters are memorable. (Orlando: Harcourt, Brace, Jovanovich, 1984)

Sarah, Plain and Tall by *Patricia MacLachlan*   (8 - 12)

Caleb and Anna conjure up memories of their mother, who died the day Caleb was born. They long for their mother's songs and the life she brought to their home and their father. Then Papa decides to place an advertisement in the newspaper for a "mail order bride." Sarah Elisabeth Wheaton of Maine answers the ad and decides to come to visit for a month. Unsure beginnings transform to more solid commitments and the promise of creating a satisfying family life together, as Sarah brings the gift of celebration back into their lives. (New York: Harper Trophy, 1985)

Mieko and the Fifth Treasure by *Eleanor Coerr*   (9 - 12)

The author of *Sadako and the Thousand Paper Cranes* brings this story of a girl who paints Japanese words. She paints with four treasures: a sable brush, an ink stick, an ink stone, and rice paper. Her art teacher tells her she possesses a fifth treasure: beauty in her heart. When Mieko is a victim of the bomb that devastates Nagasaki, she is badly hurt and is left with a scarred hand. She must overcome her bitterness and anger and find inner peace once again. (New York: G.P. Putnam's Sons, 1993)

Bridge to Teribithia by *Katherine Paterson*   (10 - 12)

Jess Aaron experiences the meaning of friendship and intimacy when he and a new fifth grader, Leslie Burke, become "best friends." Leslie not only inspires Jess's imagination through the creation of a magical kingdom in the forest, but also shows him that parents need not be strangers and adversaries. (New York: Harper Trophy, 1977)

A Peacemaking Tale to Spin

"The Old Man and His Grandson"

Once there was an old man who lived with his son, his daughter-in-law, and his four-year-old grandson. The poor, old man was nearly blind and deaf, and his knees and hands trembled terribly. When he sat with the rest of the family around the table at mealtime, his hands shook so much that it took a great deal of effort just to hold his spoon. He spilled his soup on the tablecloth and dribbled it down his chin. His son and daughter-in-law were sick with the sight of him, and they made the old man sit behind the stove where they could not see the mess he made. They brought him little bits of food in a clay bowl — not nearly enough to fill his aching belly. The old man sat behind the stove with tears in his eyes.

One day, the old man's hands shook so much that he dropped the bowl, and it broke at his feet. His son and daughter-in-law pointed their fingers and scolded him, but the old man did not wish to fight. All he wanted was a good, warm meal. Finally, the son and daughter-in-law bought him a wooden bowl for mealtime, so that it would not break.

As they were sitting about after dinner one night, the grandson was stacking some wooden pieces.

"What are you doing, son?" his father asked.

"I am building a trough," the lad replied, "so that you and mother may eat out of it when you are old."

The two parents looked at one another and burst into tears over what they had done. After that, Grandfather always had a special place at the table, and whenever he spilled, there was never an unkind word spoken.

(A Grimms' tale, retold by Shea Darian)

Conclusion

A Parenting Covenant

Parenting calls us toward a new meaning of servanthood. There is no job on the face of the planet that requires more of our hands, heart, or mind. The demands of this path call for tangible symbols to empower us with our visions of whole parenting and meaningful family life.

Of all the challenges I have encountered, none has been greater than the constant unfolding of my identity as a parent. Just when I think I have a handle on it, our children move on to a new stage of development, and I must learn over again how to be with them and provide an environment of nourishment. In my search for clarity amidst these constant changes, I have found it important to ask myself what I most wish to offer my children through all the phases and stages of these growing years.

When Morgan was a baby, Andrew and I wrote a parenting covenant that has been a beacon for us, as we attempt to live out our parenting ideals. We spoke this covenant for the first time at Morgan's baptism when she was nine months old and spoke it again to both our children at Willa's baptism when she was three. For us, this covenant has been a stronghold of encouragement. It is a tangible symbol of all that compelled us to become parents in the first place. And during times when our ideals seem buried under our efforts, our own words call out to us, reminding us of our vision and purpose:

Morgan and Willa, we create this covenant as your *grand*parents. [Tage]

We promise to love you with a transforming love,
a love that accepts you as you are unconditionally.

We promise to comfort you in your pain and vulnerability,
and to celebrate with you in your joy and discovery.

We promise to teach you
what we believe it means to be strong and humane
and to seek peace in our family and in our world.
We promise to share with you our insights of Life,
realizing that you will grow
into your own insights, choices, and unique ways of being.

We respect the person you are forever becoming
and promise to learn from you all you have to teach us.

We promise to play with you,
to work side-by-side with you,
to cry with you and laugh with you.

And as we learn to *guide* parent and love you,
we dedicate ourselves to learning, more fully,
what it means to parent *nurture you*
and to love ourselves and each other.

Appendices & Indices

Examples of Daily and Weekly Family Rhythms

The preceding chapters include a number of simple ritual ideas, any of which you may choose to transform into a cherished family rhythm by approaching it with awareness and regularity. By now, you may be bubbling over with ideas about how you can make your family life a more rhythmic experience. Or you may be more able to identify some rhythmic elements already existing in your family life upon which you may build.

For the very busy, and those coming to the idea of rhythm for the first time, I remind you to *begin where you are and consider only one change for your family at a time.* If you have been familiar with the experience of creating rhythm in your family life for some time, you may wish to carry the experience still further . . . it is for such folks that I am including the following examples of daily and weekly family rhythms. They are not prescriptions. They are meant to be catalysts to spur the creation of your own rhythms that will meet your family's unique needs and interests.

It is important when developing a more comprehensive, intentional approach to rhythm not to forget spontaneity. Utilize your rhythmic sketch of family life as a foundation upon which you can rely, but which is not meant to preclude the spontaneity, craziness, and unforeseen adventures that are sure to come along from time to time. Also, remember to reassess your family needs occasionally and alter your rhythms as necessary — once more, a bit at a time.

Example #1: A parent who stays home with child/ren, or parents who share this responsibility

Daily Weekday Rhythms:

- Waking, Dressing, and Breakfast
- Household Chores (child engages in free-play and weaves into adult's activity occasionally)
- Mid-morning Snack
- Outdoor Time (or running necessary errands)
- Lunch
- Storytime
- Quiet Time/Naptime
- Mid-afternoon Snack
- Baking, Crafting, Preparing Food (for dinner)
- Dinner
- Family Time (if spouse, parenting partner, siblings, or extended family has returned home)

- Personal Time for Primary Parent (if possible, time during which spouse, parenting partner, grandparent, etc. shares time with child, perhaps moving into bedtime ritual)
- Bedtime Ritual for Child
- Personal Time or Intimate Time (with spouse or friend)

Weekly Rhythms

- Tuesday Morning — library
- Thursday Morning — playgroup with other parents and children
- Saturday Evening — a time for parent/s to play (obtain childcare provider)

Example #2: Family in which parent/s work/s outside the home (child/ren are school age or in childcare situation)

Daily Weekday Rhythms

- Family Breakfast
- Depart for School/Childcare and Work
- Return Home
- Greeting (share a few intimate moments before dinner preparation)
- Prepare Dinner (older child may help; you may wish to set younger child up with a special activity or allow them to do a simple task in the preparation nearby you; if there are two adults in the household the most ideal plan may be for one to share intimate moments with the child/ren, while the other gets dinner ready)
- Dinner
- Family Time (to go for a walk, to the park, or for reading together)
- Bedtime Ritual for Children
- Personal Time or Intimate Time (with spouse or friend)

Weekly Rhythms

- Saturday Morning — plan meals and buy food for the week
- Sunday Morning — church gathering
- Sunday Afternoon — special family time

Great Books for Parents

Wading through the myriad of parenting books available can be time-consuming. Here are some rare gems I have encountered, which you may find useful.

Arts & Crafts

The Children's Year: Crafts and Clothes for Children and Parents to Make by Stephanie Cooper, Christine Fynes-Clinton, and Marye Rowling

> If I could have only one craft book in my library, this would be it. Over 100 craft instructions are included in seasonal groupings, which inspire greater awareness and celebration for the turning of the seasons. Natural materials are used to make toys, dolls, clothing, and seasonal symbols. (Stroud, UK: Hawthorn Press, 1986)

The Doll Book: Soft Dolls and Creative Free Play by Karin Neuschutz

> This book offers an excellent discussion of child development as it relates to play, and the special role dolls hold in the life of the child. Detailed instructions are given for creating knot-dolls, sack dolls, coverall dolls, yarn dolls, and dress-up dolls from natural fabrics. (New York: Larson Publishing, Inc., 1982)

Earth, Water, Fire, and Air: Playful Explorations in the Four Elements by Walter Kraul

> A craft book for older children, which includes such projects as waterwheels, parachutes, and spinning tops. (Edinburgh: Floris, 1989)

Echoes of a Dream: Creative Beginnings for Parent and Child by Susan Smith

> This book proves that big things may come in small packages. If you do not have much time for reading, this little treasure will fuel your creative fires with ideas on gardening, cooking, crafts, toys, watercolor painting, and drawing with crayons. (London, Ontario: Waldorf School Association of London, 1982)

Make Your Own Musical Instruments by Muriel Mandell and Robert E. Wood

> From rhythm sticks to cymbals, bells to drums, this "oldie but goodie" offers a myriad of projects for homemade instruments. (New York: Sterling Publishing Co., Inc., 1957)

The Nature Corner by M. van Leeuwen and J. Moeskops

> An inspired resource for creating a nature corner with your child. (Edinburgh: Floris, 1990)

Painting with Children by Brunhild Muller

> A guide for parents and teachers on bringing the art of watercolor painting to children. Includes information on Goethe's color theory and the effect of colors on children. (Edinburgh: Floris Books, 1987)

Snips & Snails & Walnut Whales: Nature Crafts for Children by Phyllis Fiarotta

> Over 100 projects for children and parents to make from such natural materials as pinecones, stones, seeds, leaves, and flowers. (New York: Workman Publ. Co., 1975)

Toymaking with Children by Freya Jaffke

> An excellent collection of toys to make from natural materials. (Edinburgh: Floris Books, 1988)

Cooking & Nutrition

Cooking for Consciousness: Whole Food Recipes for the Vegetarian Kitchen by Joy McCloure and Kendall Layne.

> A natural foods cookbook that includes eggless baked goods, natural sweeteners, and instructions for making your own tofu, yogurt, sour cream, and more . . . A wealth of information. (Willow Springs, MO: Nucleus Publications, 1993)

Eating for a Fresh Start by Marcia Singer

> A resource for children grades 1 - 7 (and the whole family), which offers helpful information for beginning vegetarians. Easy to follow instructions are given for sprouting, food combining, good digestion practices, and great recipes. The book includes facts about how our eating habits affect animals and the environment. (Los Angeles: P. L. A. Y. House, 1990)

Feeding the Whole Family: Down-to-Earth Cookbook and Whole Foods Guide by Cynthia Lair

> This book will help you convert your family to a whole foods way of life. Intelligent nutritional information complements sensible solutions for preparing family meals, quick dinners, lunch boxes, and children's treats. Also includes tips for attracting children to wholesome foods. (San Diego: LuraMedia, 1994)

Vegetarian Cooking Around the World by Robert L. Wolfe and Diane Wolfe

> Intended for the older elementary child as well as the teenager. Contains easy recipes for cooking ethnic dishes. (Minneapolis: Lerner Publications Company, 1992)

The Vegetarian Lunchbasket: 225 easy, nutritious recipes for the quality conscious family on the go by Linda Haynes

> A book you'll turn to again and again. Includes 60 sandwich combinations, soup and thermos items, salads, main dishes, desserts, and snacks. (Willow Springs, MO: Nucleus Publications, 1990)

Whole Foods for the Whole Family by Roberta Johnson

> A cookbook from La Leche League International. Contains over 900 recipes, using only whole unprocessed foods and minimal amounts of salt and sweeteners. The book also contains a Kid's Cookbook section, ideas for quick meals, baby foods, and special dietary and allergy recipes. (Franklin Park, IL: La Leche League, International, 1981)

Games

Cat's Cradle, Owl's Eyes: A Book of String Games by Camilla Gryski

> An illustrated collection of 40 string games with step-by-step instructions. (New York: Beech Tree Books, 1983)

The Foxfire Book of Toys and Games edited by Linda Garland Page and Hilton Smith

> A fun-filled collection of Appalachian games and crafts, with photos and interviews of Appalachian folks who contributed. (New York: Dutton, 1985)

Hopscotch, Hangman, Hot Potato, & Ha Ha Ha: A Rulebook of Children's Games by Jack Maguire

> A collection of more than 250 games with step-by-step instructions. (New York: Prentice Hall Press, 1990)

***The New Games Book* and *More New Games!* edited by Andrew Fluegelman**

> Both of these volumes offer a well-spring of cooperative games for hours of fun. (Garden City: Dolphin Books, 1976/1981)

***Step It Down: Games, Plays, Songs & Stories from the Afro-American Heritage* by Bessie Jones and Bess Lomax Hawes**

> A delightful collection for children of all ages. (Athens: The University of Georgia Press, 1987)

Also under "Songbooks" see *American Folksongs for Children* and *Shake It to the One That You Love the Best.*

Gardening

***Gardening with Peter Rabbit* by Jennie Walters (Illustrations by Beatrix Potter)**

> A fun-filled collection of gardening ideas through the seasons. Activities include window-sill tomatoes, new plants from old, Christmas-present bulbs, a bottle garden, and more. (London: F. Warne & Co., 1992)

***Linnea's Almanac* by Christina Bjork and Lena Anderson**

> A first-person narrative of a city girl who loves to grow things. Linnea takes us through the months of the year with gardening and craft activities, which include information about the turning of the seasons, nature, and the stars. (New York: Farrar Straus & Giroux, 1989)

***Sunflower Houses: Garden Discoveries for Children of All Ages* by Sharon Lovejoy**

> A magical offering of ideas on gardening with children. Includes information on flowers, herbs, vegetables, planning gardens, flower dolls, garden games, toys and crafts to make, and more. The simple drawings are exquisite. (Loveland, CO: Interweave Press, Inc., 1984)

***The Victory Garden Kids' Book* by Marjorie Waters**

> Step-by-step instructions which the most inexperienced gardener will appreciate. (Boston: Houghton Mifflin, 1988)

Health

***Homeopathic Medicine at Home: Natural Remedies for Everyday Ailments and Minor Injuries* by Maesimund B. Panos and Jane Heimlich**

> A helpful introduction and user's manual for treating minor ailments without drugs. (Los Angeles: Jeremy Tarcher, Inc., 1980)

***How to Raise a Healthy Child . . . In Spite of Your Doctor* by Robert S. Mendelsohn, M.D.**

> A respected pediatrician offers invaluable information concerning medical interventions, and what parents need to know to protect their children's health. The author clearly lays out the warning signs that let parents know when modern medicine is required. (New York: Random House, 1987)

Is This Your Child?: Discovering and Treating Unrecognized Allergies in Children and Adults **by Doris Rapp, M.D.**

A wealth of information on recognizing allergic symptoms and what to do about it. (New York: William Morrow, 1991)

Natural Child Care **by Maribeth Riggs**

An array of herbal home remedies for treating minor childhood illnesses. Includes a helpful section in each chapter on "When to See the Doctor." (New York: Harmony Books, 1989)

Natural Medicine for Children **by Julian Scott**

A wealth of information on such topics as herbs, homeopathy, Bach remedies, massage, and other alternative remedies for treating children from birth to age twelve. Also includes information about when it is appropriate to seek out a medical practitioner. (New York: William Morrow, 1990)

Massage

The Back Rub Book: How to Give and Receive Great Back Rubs **by Anne Kent Rush**

A wonderful resource for the whole family, with back rubs for all occasions from "A Good Morning Back Rub" to "A Birthday Back Rub." The book also includes a section on designing your own massages. (New York: Vintage Books, 1989)

The Massage Book **by George Downing**

If you want to get a bit more serious about learning massage techniques, this is an excellent resource for the beginner as well as the experienced massage-giver. In addition, this book contains instructions for a sturdy, homemade massage table. (New York: Random House, 1972)

Nature & the Environment

Fifty Simple Things Kids Can Do to Save the Earth **by The Earth Works Group**

Experiments, facts, and activities to help make the world a cleaner, safer place. (Kansas City: Andrews and McMeel, 1990)

The Nontoxic Home **by Debra Lynn Dadd**

A wealth of information on a variety of household products from cleansers to bed linens to help protect yourself and your family from everyday toxics and health hazards. (Los Angeles: Jeremy Tarcher, Inc., 1986)

The Sense of Wonder **by Rachel Carson**

Astounding photographs are accompanied by a text that inspires adults to "help keep alive a child's inborn sense of wonder," and to awaken one's own senses to the power and beauty of nature. A delight to behold. (New York: Harper & Row, 1965)

Sharing Nature With Children **and** *Sharing the Joy of Nature* **by Joseph Cornell**

Both include activities of nature awareness for parent and child, with an age-appropriate guide. (Nevada City, CA: Dawn Publications, 1979/1989)

Parenting & Child Development

Endangered Minds: Why Children Don't Think and What We Can Do About It by Jane Healy

The author explains how our present day lifestyle prevents children from learning and developing their full potential. (New York: Simon & Schuster, 1991)

Evolutions's End by Joseph Chilton Pearce

In his ingenious observations, the author identifies five common practices in our society that hinder us from reaching our evolving potential: synthetic growth hormones, premature attempts at formal education, television, daycare, and hospital childbirth that interferes with relational bonding. (New York: HarperCollins, 1992)

The Hurried Child and Miseducation: Preschoolers at Risk by David Elkind

Two indispensable volumes which consider the inappropriate pressures and expectations placed on children in our society, and the potentially devastating outcomes of this "hurried" approach. (New York: Alfred A. Knopf, 1984/1987)

Lifeways: Working with Family Questions compiled by Gundrun Davy and Bons Voors

A helpful collection of essays by various authors on children, family life, balancing parenting with personal fulfillment. Although one major section of the book is devoted specifically to Christian festivals, the remainder of the book will be an inspiration to parents from all walks of life. (Stroud, UK: Hawthorn Press, 1983)

Raising a Son: Parents and the Making of a Healthy Man by Don Elium and Jeanne Elium

Explores the challenges of raising a son in a culture that lacks intuition about fostering the healthy development of boys. (Hillsboro, OR: Beyond Words Publ., 1992)

Raising Sexually Healthy Children: A Loving Guide for Parents, Teachers, and Caregivers by Lynn Leight, R.N.

An invaluable resource on encouraging children with a positive view of human sexuality. Covers development from babyhood to the teen years. (New York: Avon Books, 1988)

You Are Your Child's First Teacher by Rahima Baldwin

An extraordinary resource that covers aspects of parenting and child development during the first seven years, with special insight into applying the work of Rudolf Steiner, the founder of Waldorf education. This is a book for every new parent's shelf. (Berkeley: Celestial Arts, 1989)

Poetry Collections

The Book of a Thousand Poems: A Family Treasury

A seemingly endless collection of poems selected to delight young children. Includes the works of many distinguished authors. (New York: Peter Bedrick Books, 1983)

The Golden Journey: Poems for Young People compiled by Louise Bogan and William J. Smith

This book has been noted by *The New York Times* as a book that "may well be the best general anthology of poems for young people ever compiled." From such poets as Rossetti, Frost, Tennyson, Millay, Shakespeare come treasures of verse for the whole family to enjoy. (Chicago: Contemporary Books, 1990)

I Am Phoenix **and** ***Joyful Noise*** **by Paul Fleischman**

> Both volumes contain poems for two voices, which could easily be the inspiration for a family "reader's theater." *I Am Phoenix* contains poems on various birds, while *Joyful Noise* focuses on insects. (New York: Harper & Row, 1985/1988)

Let's Do A Poem! **by Nancy Larrick**

> An inspired resource on introducing poetry to children of various ages through such tools as movement, choral reading, and drama. (New York: Delacorte Press, 1991)

Sleeping

The Family Bed **by Tine Thevenin**

> Co-family sleeping has been an accepted practice through countless generations and cultures. Today in our society it can be a heated topic of discussion. This book comes to the issue with intelligence and sensitivity. (Garden City Park, NY: Avery Publ., 1987)

Nighttime Parenting: How to Get Your Baby and Child Asleep **by William Sears, M.D.**

> An excellent resource that explains the sleeping patterns of babies, and how parents may lower the risk of Sudden Infant Death Syndrome. (Franklin Park, IL: La Leche League International, 1985)

Songbooks

American Folk Songs for Children **by Ruth Crawford Seeger**

> An illustrated collection of over 90 folksongs for the whole family to enjoy, including work songs, ballads, chants, and spirituals. (New York: Doubleday & Co., Inc., 1948)

A Circle is Cast **and** ***Fire Within*** **compiled by Libana**

> Beautiful collections of sacred songs. Mostly rounds, but may be sung in unison with young children.These songs reflect gratitude for the seasons and the earth. Tapes are also available, which might be an aid for those unable to read music. Order from: Libana, P.O. Box 530, Cambridge, MA. 02140. (Cambridge, MA: Libana, Inc., 1986/Durham, N.C.: Ladyslipper, Inc., 1990)

Pentatonic Songs **by Elizabeth Lebret**

> A collection of songs in the pentatonic scale, especially appropriate for nursery, kindergarten, first-, and second-grade children. (Thornhill, Ontario: The Waldorf School Association of Ontario, 1985)

Rise Up Singing **edited by Peter Blood-Patterson**

> The lyrics to over 1200 songs old and new, including a "play" section especially for youngsters. (Bethlehem, PA: Sing Out Corporation, 1988)

Shake It to the One That You Love the Best: Play Songs and Lullabies from Black Musical Traditions **collected and adapted by Cheryl Warren Mattox**

> A wonderful collection of timeless favorites, which includes illustrations by two contemporary African-American artists, Varnette P. Honeywood and Brenda Joys-mith. (El Sobrante, CA: Warren-Mattox Productions, 1989)

***Shepard's Songbook: For Grades I, II, and III of Waldorf Schools* by Elisabeth Lebret**

A lovely collection of songs for lower elementary children, which includes information on the pentatonic scale, music theory, and appropriate music and teaching methods for this age group. (Private edition, available through the Waldorf Institute, 260 Hungry Hollow Rd., Spring Valley, NY 10977)

***Songs of the Earth* written and compiled by Anne Kealoha**

A useful collection of sacred songs from a variety of spiritual traditions, including African, Buddhist, Christian, Jewish, Sufi, and more. (Berkeley: Celestial Arts, 1989)

Storytelling

***The Art of the Storyteller* by Marie L. Shedlock**

A wealth of information for the aspiring storyteller. (New York: Dover)

***The Feminine in Fairytales* by M.L. von Franz**

An excellent lecture series considering the problems of the feminine in fairytales, which will prompt the reader toward a deeper understanding of feminine imagery in tales and the implications. (Dallas: Spring Publications, Inc., 1972)

***The Uses of Enchantment: The Meaning and Importance of Storytelling* by Bruno Bettelheim**

A profound account of the value of fairytales for children. (New York: Random House, 1977)

Story Collections

***Best-Loved Folktales of the World* by Joanna Cole**

A wonderful collection that will bring pleasure for the whole family. (Garden City, NY: Doubleday, 1982)

***The Complete Grimm's Fairy Tales* by Padraic Colum, and commentary by Joseph Campbell**

With 200 tales to choose from, one is sure to find a few that will delight! (New York: Pantheon, 1972)

***The Indian Way: Learning to Communicate with Mother Earth* by Gary McLain**

A book of stories and activities for children 8 and up, which focus on the eve of each full moon, when Grandpa Iron (a Northern Arapahoe medicine man) gathers his grandchildren to tell them stories of wisdom about the earth, plants, animals, our homes, and more. (Santa Fe: John Muir Publications, 1990)

***Keepers of the Earth* and *Keepers of the Animals* by Michael Caduto and Joseph Bruchac**

Two intriguing collections of tales and activities focusing on creation. The authors utilize creative arts, math, sensory awareness, social studies and writing to foster environmental awareness and responsibility. Particular activities are defined as appropriate for younger children (5-8) and older children (9-12). (Golden, CO: Fulcrum, Inc. 1988/1991)

The Maid of the North: Feminist Folktales from Around the World **by Ethel Johnston Phelps**
> These wondrous tales are captivating and reflect strength in the women as well as the men. (New York: Henry Holt & Co., 1981)

The People Could Fly: American Black Folktales **told by Virginia Hamilton**
> A collection that includes notes about each story and demonstrates the significance of the art of storytelling to the Afro-American culture, especially as it relates to slavery and emancipation. (New York: Alfred A. Knopf, 1985)

Television & Electronic Media

Four Arguments for the Elimination of Television **by Jerry Mander**
> This book will motivate parents to take a long look at TV time for their children. (New York: Morrow, 1978)

The Plug-in Drug and Unplugging the Plug-in Drug **by Marie Winn**
> The first volume, which includes information about video games and computers, is an excellent study of television addiction in children. The second volume offers a myriad of ideas for alternatives to TV time. (New York: Viking Penguin, Inc., 1985/1987)

Who's Bringing Them Up? How to Break the TV Habit! **by Martin Large**
> A practical guide for control and elimination of TV viewing time. (Stroud, UK: Hawthorn, 1990)

Also under "Parenting & Child Development" see *Endangered Minds*.

Waldorf Education & Parenting

Confessions of a Waldorf Parent **by Margaret Gorman**
> An enlightening and humorous account of the author's joys and challenges in meeting and embracing Waldorf education. (Fair Oaks, CA: Rudolf Steiner College Publications, 1990)

Creativity in Education **by Rene Querido**
> An introductory overview of the motivations and methods of Waldorf education. (San Francisco: H.S. Dakin, 1982)

Kingdom of Childhood **by Rudolf Steiner**
> A lecture series given by the founder of Waldorf education in 1924, which is full of insight on the developing child, especially in relation to classroom work. (Hudson, NY: Anthroposophic Press, 1982)

Steiner Education in Theory and Practice **by Gilbert Childs**
> An excellent resource on Rudolf Steiner's view of the developing child, as well as the Waldorf school curriculum and teaching methods. (Edinburgh: Floris, 1992)

Also under "Parenting & Child Development" see *Lifeways* and *You Are Your Child's First Teacher*.

Resources for Parents

There are a number of useful parenting resource groups and suppliers. Below I have listed a few of them. Most of the mail order suppliers have free catalogs available for the asking.

Books

Chinaberry Book Service
2780 Via Orange Way, Suite B
Spring Valley, CA 91978
800-776-2242

> A mail-order book service that offers a free catalog seasonally. Includes a myriad of quality children's books, as well as "good reads" for parents. The book reviews are almost as fun to read as the books.

Hearts and Hands
637 Bunting Dr.
Delray Beach, FL 33444
407-272-8298

> A catalog of books and playthings for children. The books feature realistic portrayals of African Americans in everyday settings.

Informed Birth and Parenting
Box 3675
Ann Arbor, MI 48106
313-662-6857

> Offers a small but excellent selection of books on birth, early childhood, parenting, and Waldorf education. Also offers videos on birth and midwifery.

Mother & Home Books
Westerdale Rd.
RR 2 Box 122
Woodstock, VT 05091
802-457-1993

> A book service offering hard-to-find books and tools for parents (dads are included too). If you have ever thought, "Someone should write a book on . . . ," you may find it here! These resources are sure to inspire fun and creativity in your parenting.

Also under "Toys & Games" see Hearthsong, who is now publishing a book catalog.

Gardening

Seeds of Change
1364 Rufina Circle #5
Santa Fe, NM 87501
505-438-8080

> Offering organic seeds for growing herbs and vegetables.

Shepherd's Garden Seeds
30 Irene Street
Torrington, CT 06790
203-482-3638

> Offers a fine assortment of seeds for flowers, herbs, and vegetables, plants and tubers, as well as cooking and gardening supplies. An organic gardener I know says these seeds grow some of the tastiest vegetables he's ever eaten.

Homeschooling

Holt Associates
2269 Massachusetts Ave.
Cambridge, MA 02140
617-864-3100

> Offers a magazine called "Growing Without Schooling," also pamphlets, a directory of associated homeschoolers, and more.

Home Education Press
PO Box 1083
Tonasket, WA 98855

> Offers a journal, articles, and other materials on homeschooling.

The Moore Foundation
Box 1
Camas, WA 98607
206-835-2736

> Embraces the spiritual and social aspects of home education as well as the more traditional aspects. Also offers a newsletter.

National Homeschool Association
PO Box 290
Hartland, MI 48353-0290
313-632-5208

> A useful networking resource, which also offers a newsletter.

Oak Meadow
Box 712
Blacksburg, VA 24063
703-552-3263

> Offers an independent Waldorf-inspired homeschooling curriculum for grades K-12.

Journals

Childhood
RR 1, Box 2675
Westford, VT 05494
802-879-4869

> A quarterly publication that brings a Waldorf approach to the arts of parenting, schooling, and homeschooling.

Mothering
PO Box 1690 DIHB
Santa Fe, NM 87504
505-984-8116

> A quarterly magazine that focuses on alternative approaches to pregnancy and birth, parenting, education, child development, health, and family life.

Parenting for Peace & Justice Newsletter
Institute for Peace and Justice
4144 Lindell Blvd.
St. Louis, MO 63104
314-533-4445

> An international interfaith network for parents who wish to work toward a healthy family life in which social ministry is a priority.

Peridot
921 SW Depot Ave.
Gainesville, FL 32601
904-375-6291

> "A journal for creative educational ideas." Published by the Waldorf School of Gainesville to promote the education and development of the whole child.

Musical Instruments

Choroi
Karen Klaveness
4600 Minnesota Ave.
Fair Oaks, CA 95628
916-966-1227

> Offers a selection of kinderharps, pentatonic and diatonic flutes, and more.

Harps of Lorien
Raphael and Lorna Weisman
610 North Star Route
Questa, NM 97556
505-586-1307

> A wide selection of harps for the whole family, as well as dulcimers, bagpipes, sitars, guitars, violins, recorders, pentatonic flutes, harmonicas, drums, percussion and more.

Song of the Sea
Anne and Edward Damm
47 West Street
Bar Harbor, ME 04609
207-288-5653

> Offers kinderharps, recorders, dulcimers, drums, folk toys, and more.

Natural Clothing & Household Products

Coyote Found Candles
PO Box 632
Port Townsend, WA 98368
206-385-4142 (or for orders call 800-788-4142)

> Offers beeswax candles, holders, candle decorating supplies, and more.

Lehman's Hardware and Appliances, Inc.
4779 Kidron Road
PO Box 41
Kidron, OH 44636
216-857-5441

> Offers a vast selection of old-fashioned merchandise such as butter churns, iron skillets, toys, and clothes drying racks, as well as some newfangled stuff like composting toilets.

The Natural Baby Company
114 W. Franklin, Suite S
Pennington, NJ 08534
609-737-2895
> Natural clothing, nursing wear, books, and toys.

The Natural Choice
Eco Design Co.
1365 Rufina Circle
Santa Fe, NM 87501
505-438-3448
> Household and personal care products, clothing, natural paints and wood stains, and more.

Richman Cotton Company
529 Fifth St.
Santa Rosa, CA 95401
800-992-8924
> An unpretentious selection of no-nonsense natural clothing for the whole family, as well as toys, crafts, and more.

Seventh Generation
Colchester, VT 05446-1672
800-456-1177
> An excellent selection of home and personal care products, as well as clothing for the whole family.

Biobottoms: Fresh Air Wear for Kids
P.O. Box 6009
Detaluma, CA 94953
800-766-1254
> Natural clothing for children, infant to pre-teen.

Garnet Hill: The Original Natural Fibers Catalogue
262 Main St.
Franconia, NH 03580-0262
800-622-6216
> Natural Fibers for home and family.

Organizations for Parents

Informed Birth and Parenting
Box 3675
Ann Arbor, MI 48106
313-662-6857
> An excellent resource in the areas of pregnancy, birth, midwifery, and the Waldorf approach to parenting and education.

La Leche League International
PO Box 1209
Franklin Park, IL 60131-8209
708-455-7730
> A significant resource for parents, offering information on pregnancy, birth, breastfeeding, and awareness in parenting.

Mothers at Home
Dept. MHB7
8310 A Old Courthouse Rd.
Vienna, VA 22182
800-783-4MOM
> Support network for at-home moms. Publishes journal called "Welcome Home."

Toys, Dolls, & Games

Major mail-order sources:

Animal Town
PO Box 485
Healdsburg, CA 95448
800-445-8642
> Cooperative games, toys, and books on cooperation and family activities.

Hearthsong
PO Box B
Sebastopol, CA 95473-0601
800-325-2502
> Toys, books, games, beeswax, beeswax crayons, and more.

Smaller, more personal sources:

A Child's Dream
PO Box 1427
Lyons, CO 80540
800-359-2906

Kottage Kids
5464 Rabe Rd.
Columbia Falls, MT 59912
406-387-5828

Magic Cabin Dolls
PO Box 64
Viroqua, WI 54665
608-637-2735

Waldorf Education

Association of Waldorf Schools of North
America
3750 Bannister Road
Fair Oaks, CA 95628
916-961-0927
> Publishes journal, also offers a listing of Waldorf schools throughout the world, and part-time teacher training programs available.

The Magical Years Conference
Rudolf Steiner School of Ann Arbor
2775 Newport Rd.
Ann Arbor, MI 48103
313-995-4141
> An annual weekend conference in the spring for Waldorf parents and teachers.

Rudolf Steiner College
9200 Fair Oaks Boulevard
Fair Oaks, CA 95628
916-961-8727
> Full-time teacher training program, summer and weekend workshops offered. Also home of St. George Book Service, which offers a selection of books on Waldorf education and parenting.

Waldorf Institute of Sunbridge College
260 Hungry Hollow Rd.
Spring Valley, NY 10977
914-425-0055
> Full-time teacher training program, summer and weekend workshops, and bookstore. Also sponsors a teacher training extension program at the Chicago Waldorf School in Chicago, IL.

Verse Index

Alphabetical Title Listing

Song Index

Alphabetical Title Listing

Song Index

Pentatonic Songs

Rounds

Storybook/Folk Tale Index

Alphabetical Title Listing

Storybook/Folk Tale Index

Age-Appropriate Listing

The broad age ranges for the storybooks reflect the possibility of divergent uses. While books like Dreamcatcher, Cornrows, and The Way to Start a Day can be delightful stories for the young ones, they can also provide older children with historical information and expose them to exceptional artwork that might be a springboard for their own endeavors. My choices for age-appropriateness were influenced by the tone of the narrative voice and subject matter.

---

* Choose stories to tell according to your child's age. While "The Magic Porridge Pot" and "The Star Money" may be chosen for younger children, "The Boy Who Learned to Listen" and "A Riddling Tale" will be more appropriate for an older child.

Photograph by Chara Gail Holt.

The youngest of four children, **Shea Darian** was born in Jefferson City, Missouri, and raised in Urbandale, Iowa. She received her B.A. in Speech Communications and Theatre from Iowa State University and her Master of Divinity degree from Garrett Evangelical Seminary. Shea was ordained in the United Methodist Church and has served as youth minister, minister to singles, and minister through the arts. She is a singer and songwriter, contemporary liturgist and ritual-maker. Living in Louisville, Kentucky, with her spouse and two children, Shea presently serves as administrator for the Waldorf School of Louisville.

Other LuraMedia Publications

BANKSON, MARJORY ZOET

Braided Streams:
Esther and a Woman's Way of Growing

Seasons of Friendship:
Naomi and Ruth as a Pattern

"This Is My Body. . .":
Creativity, Clay, and Change

BORTON, JOAN

Drawing from the Women's Well: *Reflections on the Life Passage of Menopause*

CARTLEDGE-HAYES, MARY

To Love Delilah:
Claiming the Women of the Bible

DARIAN, SHEA

Seven Times the Sun:
Guiding Your Child through the Rhythms of the Day

DOHERTY, DOROTHY ALBRACHT
and **McNAMARA, MARY COLGAN**

Out of the Skin Into the Soul:
The Art of Aging

DUERK, JUDITH

Circle of Stones:
Woman's Journey to Herself

I Sit Listening to the Wind:
Woman's Encounter within Herself

GOODSON, WILLIAM (with Dale J.)

Re-Souled: *Spiritual Awakenings of a Psychiatrist and his Patient in Alcohol Recovery*

JEVNE, RONNA FAY

It All Begins With Hope:
Patients, Caretakers, and the Bereaved Speak Out

The Voice of Hope:
Heard Across the Heart of Life

with ALEXANDER LEVITAN
No Time for Nonsense:
Getting Well Against the Odds

KEIFFER, ANN

Gift of the Dark Angel: *A Woman's Journey through Depression toward Wholeness*

LAIR, CYNTHIA

Feeding the Whole Family: *Down-to-Earth Cookbook and Whole Foods Guide*

LODER, TED

Eavesdropping on the Echoes:
Voices from the Old Testament

Guerrillas of Grace:
Prayers for the Battle

Tracks in the Straw:
Tales Spun from the Manger

Wrestling the Light:
Ache and Awe in the Human-Divine Struggle

MEYER, RICHARD C.

One Anothering: *Biblical Building Blocks for Small Groups*

NELSON, G. LYNN

Writing & Being: *Taking Back Our Lives through the Power of Language*

O'HALLORAN, SUSAN *and* **DELATTRE, SUSAN**

The Woman Who Lost Her Heart:
A Tale of Reawakening

PRICE, H.H.

Blackberry Season:
A Time to Mourn, A Time to Heal

RAFFA, JEAN BENEDICT

The Bridge to Wholeness:
A Feminine Alternative to the Hero Myth

Dream Theatres of the Soul:
Empowering the Feminine through Jungian Dreamwork

ROTHLUEBBER, FRANCIS

Nobody Owns Me: *A Celibate Woman Discovers her Sexual Power*

RUPP, JOYCE

The Star in My Heart:
Experiencing Sophia, Inner Wisdom

SAURO, JOAN

Whole Earth Meditation:
Ecology for the Spirit

SCHNEIDER-AKER, KATHERINE

God's Forgotten Daughter:
A Modern Midrash: What If Jesus Had Been A Woman?

WEEMS, RENITA J.

I Asked for Intimacy: *Stories of Blessings, Betrayals, and Birthings*

Just a Sister Away: *A Womanist Vision of Women's Relationships in the Bible*

LURAMEDIA™

LuraMedia, Inc.
7060 Miramar Rd., Suite 104
San Diego, CA 92121

Books for Healing and Hope,
Balance and Justice
Call 1-800-FOR-LURA for information.